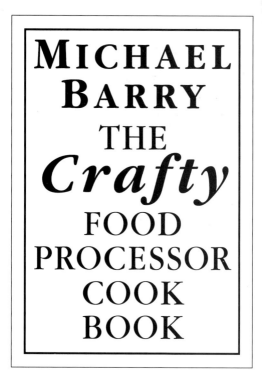

Michael Barry

THE *Crafty* FOOD PROCESSOR COOK BOOK

JARROLD

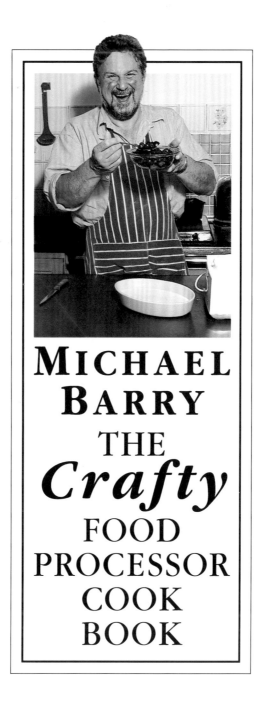

MICHAEL BARRY

THE *Crafty* FOOD PROCESSOR COOK BOOK

JARROLD

The Crafty Food Processor Cook Book

Recipes – Michael Barry
Food for photography – The Banham Bakehouse, Norfolk
Food styling – Georgina Harris
Photography – Denis Avon
Designer – Geoff Staff
Editor – Helen Thompson

Designed and produced by Parke Sutton Limited, Norwich
for Jarrold Publishing, Norwich

ISBN 0-7117-0565-8

Printed in England

Contents

Introduction to food processor cookery

the processor method. And that is what I am going to do all the way through this book, because for me, after good knives, a food processor is perhaps the most fundamental tool in my kitchen. I use it all the time – not just for major things like mincing meat or kneading bread, but for chopping herbs, making a salad dressing creamy, for slicing a cucumber wafer-thin to make a lovely sweet and sour salad, to make a delicious *hollandaise* to eat with fresh asparagus, or to purée mangos for a scrumptuous fool. These are all things I can think of doing casually as an everyday part of cooking rather than for special occasions, simply because I use the food processor.

A word of caution! By and large almost anything a food processor does *can* be done by hand, although much more slowly, and with a lot more effort. But there are some things I am not sure hand cooking would provide. There are soups that can be made so velvety smooth I dread to think how many times they would have to

When I wrote the first edition of this book some twelve years ago, I began it by saying 'welcome to the great processor revolution'. At that time, food processors were virtually brand new and were only just beginning to replace the liquidisers or mixers that people had been using in their kitchens for years, and microwaves still seemed to represent the kind of weapon science fiction hero Dan Dare could use to eliminate Martian enemies. Things have changed a lot since then, and food processors are much cheaper and widely available from a considerable number of manufacturers in a wide range of sizes and capacities. What hasn't changed, though, is how big a difference a food processor can make to your cooking. There are a whole lot of dishes that these days no one, not even a professional chef, would consider trying to make without a food processor. Indeed many of the top French chefs now write cookery books that presume that you will use a food processor as a normal part of your cooking equipment. They don't begin with the hand method and say you can also make things with a processor, they begin with pass through a sieve to achieve the same results by hand; and the most accurate cutter in the world using a perfect knife would have enormous difficulty in making the identically sized mass slices of carrot or courgette that the French called *Juliennes* but I prefer to call the old English name of spillikins. One of the cutters on your food processor can produce them. A processor, then, is not just for special occasions, although it is worth having simply for the special dishes it helps you produce. It is also for everyday cooking. I find I now use it casually without planning or thinking about it, just as I would any other fundamendal tool, because that's what it is – not a gadget but a tool. There was a time, as I said in the first edition, that there were things that a processor wouldn't do well – it wouldn't whisk egg whites, it wouldn't juice oranges or make mashed potatoes without turning them into glue. With modern processors, none of those difficulties exists any more although you need to make sure you have got the correct fitting to provide the desired result.

Having said all that, I don't think that food processors are the only useful things in the kitchen or that everything should be done in them. There are lots of things that I still do by hand – beating eggs for an omelette or slicing tomatoes, for instance – but there is no question that a food processor really does improve the quality and range of your cooking quite enormously, and that also applies to things you are really quite good at doing already. It wasn't until I kneaded bread with mine that I discovered just how close and firm and well risen bread could be when you kneaded it with a food processor instead of by hand. The machine has, of course, the great advantage of being able to make left-overs into the most amazing soups, pâtés and dips.

What I hope this book will do is show you how you can use a food processor for everyday and special occasion meals. There are detailed recipes, suggestions, tips and ideas but they are all really just the beginning because most of the food you cook can be enhanced, helped or made easier by using a food processor. This is not a comprehensive list of all that a food processor can do, it is just a collection of my favourite recipes. I hope that you will find the opportunity to use your own favourites too.

A basic guide to the food processor

Do make friends with your food processor. It may look quite complicated and difficult at first and there may seem to be lots of bits and pieces that you are sure you are never going to use, but it is worthwhile putting it together and taking it apart a few times until you feel comfortable and understand it. Do be careful though – some of the blades are very sharp in order to do their jobs.

Let me take you through the whole process step by step. First of all, every processor, whatever its make, has a motor section. This provides the power and has one or two different kinds of motor in it. What some people consider the best, the strongest and the quietest is the direct drive motor, a very heavy motor with only one moving part. It produces constant speed, whatever the load put on it, and it delivers an adjusted amount of power to keep the blades moving at the same rotation, usually around 1000 rotations per minute. The other kind varies the speed of the blades, which is either done by a switch or depends on the load put on it. It normally begins at a much higher speed – up to 2000–2500 rotations a minute – and slows down as the work load increases. Almost all processors have a cut-out switch to prevent overloading. The instructions will tell you what to do in this situation, but it is designed to protect you so don't try to bypass it.

All processors have a transparent bowl. This comes in three pieces – the bowl itself, which carries the food or liquid that is being processed, a lid that fits tightly over the top of it, and some kind of pusher device to allow you to put foods into the feeding tube contained in the lid of the bowl without getting your fingers near the blades. Most bowls have to be fitted in a quite precise manner as a safety precaution and have to be in the right position before you can switch the power on. Do practise a few times if your processor is new to you – get the bowl on and off and make sure that it is locked into the right position.

Into the bowl go a variety of attachments. Some processors have a very basic range and some a very comprehensive one that you can build up as you go on. All of them have a double-bladed knife, rather like a miniature version of the sort of thing Boadicea might have had on her chariot, which is the key attachment and the workhorse of the system. It will chop, blend, purée, liquidise, mix, mince, knead and make pastry. It will probably also do a lot of things that I haven't thought of yet, and it shouldn't need sharpening or adjusting for many years. Most processors also have a plastic blade that looks very similar to the metal one and is used for beating and mixing batters and things like that. Some also have a plastic dough blade specially made for kneading bread but I have always found that the steel double-bladed knife has always done very well for kneading in any of the processors I have used. All processors come with a slicing disc which is designed to cut thin, regular slices from whatever is fed into the processor – cucumber, courgette, potato, apple – whatever you choose. Most slicing discs are set to produce a thin slice, and I must say I find these

most useful; but there are slicing discs that come up to half an inch in thickness for making things like potato slices for *pommes dauphinoise*. All processors also have at least one grating disc. This is an enormous advantage over any other form of grating as it not only has something to hold the food onto the grater, but unlike hand grating, there is no danger to your fingers.

Last but not least, the disc gathers all the grated ingredients in the bowl so they don't spread over the work surface as mine always seem to do. As with slicers, graters can come in a variety of sizes right up to and including a chipping disc. This not only cuts chips effortlessly and beautifully but also cuts other vegetables that you might want to have in that size for stir-frying or for stews. In between, I find the most useful size is what is called the Julienne or Coleslaw cutting disc, which produces medium-sized, long strips of vegetables, ideal again for Chinese-style cooking or for putting into salads or crudités. Egg beater discs are almost always made of white plastic with stainless steel wire beaters and are geared down to allow the eggs to gather enough air before they are beaten into total submission.

In addition there are specialist discs or attachments that fit onto some food processors. There is a fruit squeezer for use with citrus fruits, and a juicer into which you can put almost anything from carrots to grapes to produce delicious fruit juice. This is particularly useful for using up surplus or windfall fruit of which there often seems to be a glut in the autumn. In addition some food processors now have a mini-bowl that fits inside the big one if you only want to process or work with a small quantity of ingredients. Ideally this is for dealing with single portions or with small quantities of herbs which you may want to chop.

Controls

Every food processor has different controls depending on its manufacturer. All of them have a safety locking system on the lid and all of them have an on and off switch, but after that it depends on the make. Some have a pulse switch which allows you to switch on only for the length of time you hold the button down; some have a variable speed system which allows you to speed the blades up or slow down depending upon the kind of food you are working with. Some have recessed buttons, some have standing proud knobs. The only way to be sure of understanding the variety of controls you have is, once again, to put the machine together and play with it. Use your processor whenever the opportunity arises, and learn to handle it with confidence. You will find that once you get used to using it, it will save you time, trouble, energy and concern. Food processors make difficult things easy and easy things effortless. Happy crafty food processor cooking!

Tempting Dips

Dips are really an American habit which has, happily, caught on this side of the Atlantic. A variety of creamy smooth pâté type dishes, they are nicest eaten by dipping something crisp into them and putting it straight into your mouth. They are perfect with drinks before dinner, or, on a larger scale, as something to serve at a party without having to produce a full scale buffet. Dips are also something rather nice to nibble while watching the telly, or listening to your favourite record, whether it's Beethoven, Bream or the Beatles.

The best way to serve dips is in small, attractive pottery dishes with straight sides, about 1½ inches deep. The little French soufflé dishes are ideal for this, as are many of the products now being turned out by the handicraft potteries that seem to have sprung up by the hundred throughout Britain in the last few years.

To serve with them, the classic dipping tool is the crisp. However if you're a bit of a purist, why not try making your own. After all, with a processor the hard work is done for you. Just peel 2 or 3 potatoes, trim them to fit in the feed-tube, slice them, wash the slices in a little running water (you don't have to take them out of the bowl to do that); drain them and then deep fry them, a handful at a time, in hot oil just below smoking temperature – 30 seconds is enough – followed by a minute or two out of the fat, and then fry for another 45 seconds. (Don't forget to salt them before you let them cool for the second time. And if you have to store them for long make sure it's in an air-tight tin.)

If you don't fancy crisps, or there are weight-watchers about, try serving your dips with carrots, thinly sliced lengthwise (you can use the processor), chunks of celery or tiny raw cauliflower florets.

You can easily make a number of different dips because a processor makes them all in a matter of seconds. For a really show-off spread my favourites include Guacamole, Crab, and Blue Cheese and Apple. But any of them is delicious on its own. One word of warning. If you're planning to serve a meal afterwards don't serve too many or too large a portion of dips. They are surprisingly tempting.

GUACAMOLE

Guacamole is perhaps the most famous of all avocado dishes that come from Mexico, which is where the avocado was first really developed. In its homeland Guacamole is a smooth creamy complement to the very spicy dishes that so often appear on the Mexican table. The recipe below doesn't include any chilli, although if you fancy yourself as a real *compañero* you can always add a pinch. If you're feeling really *olé* try your Guacamole with the Chilli con Carné recipe on page 74.

Attachment
double-bladed knife

Ingredients
1 medium green pepper
1 small onion
3 medium tomatoes
1 large ripe avocado
2 tablespoons salad oil
1 tablespoon lemon or *fresh lime juice*
salt and pepper

Method
Cut the green pepper in half and take out all the seeds. Cut each half in four and place in the bowl together with the peeled and quartered onion, and the quartered tomatoes. Process for 5 seconds or until the vegetables are still in pieces but well cut up and mixed. Cut the avocado in half, remove the stone and keep it. Scoop out the flesh which should be soft, but not discoloured. Place it in the bowl. Add the oil and lemon or lime juice, half a teaspoon of salt, a sprinkling of black pepper and, if you fancy it, a pinch of chilli. Process for 10 seconds. Stop to scrape down the sides before processing for another 2 seconds, then pile it into a serving bowl. If you are going to store the Guacamole for more than half an hour before serving it, place the stone in the centre of the full bowl, and cover with cling film. There is a chemical in the stone that stops the avocado flesh from turning brown.

TOMATO GUACAMOLE

To make an interesting and unusual starter, reduce the number of tomatoes to one, and make as before. To serve, take a large ripe tomato for each person, cut a lid off the top about a quarter of the way down, scoop out flesh with a teaspoon, sprinkle a little salt into the tomato cases and fill with the Guacamole mixture. Put the lids back on at a jaunty angle and chill for 45 minutes before serving.

YOGHURT AND MINT

This dip is to be found under a variety of names all over the Middle East from Iran right across to Morocco. Its popularity is based on the marriage of the flavours and the cooling effect that the mint has both on spicy food and fiery climates. It's a summer dip, and one to remind you of an exotic holiday, or maybe just a romantic dream under the desert sky.

Attachment
double-bladed knife

Ingredients
¾ pint (450 ml) plain natural yoghurt (as thick as possible)
1 teaspoon salt
1 tablespoon lemon juice
6 sprigs fresh washed mint

Method
Put the yoghurt, lemon juice and salt into the bowl. Cover and process for 5 seconds until blended. Strip the mint leaves (it has to be fresh mint, dried mint just doesn't work properly with this dish) from the stalks, switch the motor on and add the leaves in two or three lots so that the first lot is completely blended into the yoghurt and the last lot still retains some semblance of separate identity. The process should take about 10 to 15 seconds. Pour into shallow bowls. In the Middle East this is often eaten using the inner leaves of a cos lettuce as spoons, an interesting and original alternative to our idea of pouring the dressing over the salad.

BLUE CHEESE AND APPLE

Cheese and apple is a favourite combination for puddings in many parts of the world. This dip combines the two and has the added attraction of a really unusual texture coming from the grated apple, whose sweetness counteracts the bite of the cheese. It's a strong, definite flavour, and one to serve on its own if you're looking for a single dip, but is equally good in the company of others.

Attachments
grating disc
double-bladed knife

Ingredients
2 eating apples
6 oz (175 g) Danish Blue cheese
½ cup milk
1 dessertspoon lemon juice
salt and pepper

Method
Core but don't peel the apples. Cut them into quarters and grate them into the bowl. Tip them out, and add the lemon juice to prevent discoloration. Fit the double-bladed knife and into the bowl (which doesn't need washing) put the broken-up blue cheese, cover and switch on. Add the milk in a slow, steady stream until the mixture blends smoothly. Put the apple back in, season, and process again for not more than 2 or 3 seconds.

FOR PHOTOGRAPH TURN TO PAGE 9 (TOP)

SOUR CREAM AND ONION

People have been known to make this dip using a packet of onion soup. Indeed, when caught short, and before food processors arrived, I have done it myself. But with a processor there are no excuses; and it's just as quick to do it the right way.

Attachment
double-bladed knife

Ingredients
1 bunch spring onions
2 chicken stock cubes
2 cartons sour cream
salt

Method
Clean the spring onions, keeping the green as well as the white parts. Cut them into 1 inch lengths; put them in the bowl. Add the chicken stock cubes, and process until they're finely chopped (7 seconds). Scrape the sides down, add the sour cream and process again until the whole mixture is amalgamated. Season to taste. When it's seasoned, pour it into its serving dish. A little of the chopped spring onions, saved before adding the sour cream, sprinkled over the top, makes a nice garnish to this lovely pale green piquant dish.

FOR PHOTOGRAPH TURN TO PAGE 9 (BOTTOM)

EGG AND TOMATO

This dip's a bit of a cheat really, because it's a version of one of my favourite sandwich fillings. In fact, if you have any left over, unlikely though that turns out to be in my experience, it does make a lovely sandwich the next day. Very cheap to make, and one of the dips that's especially popular with children, if you've got a birthday party or a picnic coming up.

Attachment
double-bladed knife

Ingredients
3 tomatoes
3 eggs
1 tablespoon butter
2 tablespoons mayonnaise (see page 35)
salt and pepper

Method
Cut the peeled tomatoes into quarters, and process for 3 or 4 seconds until roughly chopped. Scramble the eggs with butter until set but not rubbery. Take off the heat and stir in the mayonnaise. Allow to cool a moment, and then add to the bowl and process for 5 seconds more to thoroughly mix the tomatoes and egg. Season. This looks particularly pretty piled into white china dishes. It can be served with fingers of toast as an alternative to the more orthodox dipping tools.

FOR PHOTOGRAPH TURN TO PAGE 9 (LEFT)

TARAMASALATA

Originally this Eastern Mediterranean dip was made from the roe of grey mullet, but these days in Britain we make it almost exclusively from smoked cod's roe, which gives it a delicate pink flavour much to be preferred to the slightly grey colour of the original. This is also ideally eaten with hot pitta bread as part of an Eastern Mediterranean hors-d'oeuvre or 'mezze', that wonderful meal of literally tens of tiny dishes taking hours to eat and requiring gallons of conversation and beverages.

Attachment
double-bladed knife

Ingredients
6 oz (175 g) smoked cod's roe
2 slices of white bread, crusts removed
6 tablespoons of milk
juice half a lemon
2 tablespoons oil (olive is best)

Method
Pull the white bread into walnut sized pieces, place it in the processor and blend until breadcrumbs, add the milk and blend again until smooth. Put in the cod's roe cut into pieces and blend for 10–15 seconds until the mixture is smooth, add the oil and the lemon juice, blend again and taste for balance – it may need a little more lemon juice or a little more milk, depending upon the strength of the cod's roe. Put into an attractive china bowl or ramekin and chill for half an hour before serving.

HUMUS

This is a dip from the Middle East that is now becoming increasingly popular in Britain since the spread of Greek and Turkish restaurants. It is a totally vegetarian pâté with a strong garlic and lemon flavour. It is based on chick-peas, those round dried beans that you can buy in health food shops and supermarkets and need soaking for at least six hours before you cook them. They need then to be cooked for about an hour and a half. If you are making a large quantity of humus or want the totally authentic flavour and texture, this is absolutely the right way to go about it and also very economical. But if you are in a hurry you can buy tinned chick-peas in brine. They just need draining to bring them to the same point as the ones you soak and cook yourself. This particular dish is wonderful served with hot pitta bread, especially as a prelude to kebabs and salad.

Attachment
double-bladed knife

Ingredients
8 oz (225 g) soaked and cooked chick-peas
1 clove of garlic
2 tablespoons of oil (olive is best)
juice of 1 lemon
1 tablespoon tahini (sesame paste bought from health food stores)
6 tablespoons water reserved from cooking the chick peas, or freshly boiled water
1 teaspoon salt

Method
Put the oil, garlic and tahini into the mixing bowl and process for 5 seconds, add the chick-peas, lemon juice, half the water and the salt and process for 25 seconds. Scrape the sides of the bowl down, process again for 10 seconds and add the remaining water if necessary. Check for texture. If you like humus with a coarse texture it should be ready now – if you like it smoother, process again for another 10 seconds, preferably in short bursts. Put in a bowl, decorate with sprinkled paprika and chill for half an hour before serving.

CRAB DIP

This is an adaptation of a famous Cornish treat; a part of the world where the fisherman's catch and the farmer's produce blend together to make some of the most delicious food in the British Isles. It's ideal if you can get fresh or even frozen crab meat, but even if you can't, tinned will do. In the South West of England they use clotted cream in this recipe, so if you can find it, do use it. For the rest of us ordinary human beings, cottage cheese makes an adequate substitute.

Attachment
double-bladed knife

Ingredients
6 oz (175 g) cottage cheese
2 spring onions
4 tablespoons top of the milk
1 teaspoon made English mustard
6 oz (175 g) crab meat
salt and pepper

Method
Put the cottage cheese and the milk in the bowl and process until really smooth (about 15 seconds). Scrape down the sides and add the mustard, the cleaned spring onions cut into 1 inch lengths and a little salt and pepper. Process again (5 seconds) until the onion is chopped up but has not vanished. Add the crab meat, making sure to have taken out any bits of shell. Process for another 5 seconds. Pile into a serving dish and rough up the surface with a fork. It will set quite firm if left in the fridge for an hour or more.

Salsa

This is really the general name for a whole family of Mexican sauces based on raw ingredients. They are very spicy and designed to be eaten with other things although tortilla chips or corn chips make ideal scoops for a pre-drink snack. In the US, tomato salsa is very popular eaten this way. In its native country it is made just with tomatoes but with the anaemic version that we sometimes get over here you may need to add, as I suggest, a little puréed tomato from a warmer climate than our own.

Attachment
double-bladed knife

Ingredients
8 oz (225 g) ripe firm tomatoes
4 sticks spring onion
1 fresh green chilli (about the size of your little finger)
2 tablespoons salad oil
1/2 teaspoon each salt and caster sugar
2 tablespoons tomato purée (optional depending on the ripeness of tomatoes)

Method
Clean and trim the spring onions, put in the processor bowl, quarter the tomatoes and add those with all the other ingredients, including the tomato purée if needed. Split the chilli and take out all the seeds, discard the seeds and cut it into 1/2 inch sections before adding it to the bowl. Wash your hands carefully afterwards as the sting from a chilli can be transferred very easily to eyes or lips. Close the bowl and process in bursts of 2–3 seconds until the mixture is chopped but not smooth. Taste for seasoning and tip into an earthenware bowl. You can keep it in the fridge for up to 24 hours without any problems.

Fromage Frais and Walnut

Fromage frais is lovely low-fat creamy mild cheese from France which is both delicious and good for you. This recipe teams it with walnuts and garlic in an Eastern Mediterranean combination that I find particularly attractive.

Attachment
double-bladed knife

Ingredients
8 oz (225 g) fromage frais
1 clove garlic
4 oz (100 g) walnut pieces (shelled)
1 tablespoon oil (preferably walnut)
1 teaspoon salt
a sprinkling of ground nutmeg

Method
Put the peeled clove of garlic and the walnut pieces into the machine and process until the size of breadcrumbs, add the fromage frais and seasonings and process briefly again for 4–5 seconds to mix thoroughly together. You can taste the mixture at this stage – it may be that a teaspoon of lemon juice will help balance the mixture, depending on how sharp the fromage frais is. To serve, spoon into bowls and decorate with a couple of reserved walnut halves.

FOR A PRE-DINNER SNACK SERVE TOMATO SALSA WITH TORTILLA CHIPS

Country Soups

I think soup is the foundation of good food. It is almost certainly one of the earliest things people ever ate, and the great cuisines of the world, the French, the Chinese, the South East Asian, are all based on soup. For too long, we in Britain have assumed soup comes out of a tin or packet. However, for flavour, variety and economy, nothing can beat homemade soup, made delightfully easy with a food processor.

A little word about stock. In all these recipes you can use stock from ready-made chicken, beef, or vegetarian stock cubes. However, stock is not essential or even compulsory. The wonderful cook Jane Grigson came towards the end of her life to believe the flavour of stock sometimes destroyed the flavour of the ingredients in a really delicate soup and often made soups using just fresh water. Whatever you do, it is important to know that you can also make your own stock if you choose and not have to use one of the ready bought preparations. A chicken carcass simmered with a bay leaf and half an onion for an hour makes a couple of pints of such good stock that you could almost drink it on its own with a few delicate flavourings to enhance it – indeed that is what chicken noodle soup is based on. If you want a richer, darker stock made from beef or veal bones, roast first, then simmer gently to get the best flavour.

A major advantage of making soup with a processor is the variety of textures you can produce. If you want a super creamy smooth soup like vichyssoise, for example, then processing for at least a minute at full speed is the answer. If, on the other hand, you would like a country vegetable soup with the kind of texture found in France – rough grated – use a pulse technique, switching the processor on and off for brief one or two second bursts. For another kind of texture, use the grating disc to prepare the vegetables and do not process them afterwards. Any of these ways will produce a range and variety of soups I am sure you are going to love. Most of them are especially delicious when eaten with one of the homemade breads that you can find on pages 105–112.

SPINACH SOUP

This is one of those soups you can make with or without stock as you choose and you can also, if you are pushed, use frozen instead of fresh spinach. Try and buy the spinach *en branche* if you are making the frozen version as the flavour is almost always better. There is quite a generous portion of butter in this soup as well as a little milk. A lot of people believe that this is very beneficial not only for the flavour but also because it neutralises the ofalic acid that is found in fresh and cooked spinach. The soup has a very delicate flavour and a lovely colour – even those people in your family who think they hate spinach and are not Popeye fans could well be converted by this.

Attachment
double-bladed knife

Ingredients
1½ lb (675 g) fresh or 8 oz (225 g) cooked, frozen spinach
2 oz (50 g) butter
½ pint (300 ml) water
¾ pint (450 ml) milk
1 teaspoon cornflour
salt and pepper

Method
If you're using fresh spinach, wash it carefully and rough-chop it with a knife so that it's in inch wide ribbons, having discarded any tough stalks. From there on you proceed the same way whether it's fresh or frozen. Melt 1 oz (25 g) of the butter in a deep saucepan, and add the spinach. Stir to coat well with the butter. Add the water, cover the pan and simmer until the spinach is well cooked but not khaki coloured. Four to five minutes for fresh, and until it's just melted for frozen spinach, is the right length of time. Pour the spinach mixture into the processor, process for 20 seconds or until the spinach is very finely chopped indeed. You may need to stop and scrape the sides down once or twice during this process. Return the spinach purée to the pan, add the milk, having saved a little bit to mix the cornflour into a smooth paste. Add the cornflour paste, and, stirring thoroughly, bring the whole soup up gently to the boil. When it's thickened, season it well and serve it with a tiny nob of butter or a swirl of cream for each bowl. It should be pale green, flecked with little specks of darker green from the spinach leaves.

FOR PHOTOGRAPH TURN TO PAGE 15 (TOP)

POTAGE BONNE FEMME

The Good Woman's Soup – unfussy, and yet perfectly balanced, easy to do and difficult to get perfect – that is, until the food processor came along. There are a number of slight variants on this soup and my favourite version has a delicate variety of colours and a subtle blend of flavours. It's quite important not to over-process this soup as it's not meant to be completely smooth, but to have a little texture left in the vegetables.

Attachment
double-bladed knife

Ingredients
12 oz (350 g) potatoes
8 oz (225 g) carrots
8 oz (225 g) leeks
2 oz (50 g) butter
bunch of parsley
1 pint (600 ml) stock
½ pint (300 ml) milk
salt and pepper

Method
Cut all the peeled vegetables into 1 inch chunks and fry them gently in the butter in a deep saucepan until they are thoroughly coated. Add the stock, but not the milk; season and simmer for 20 minutes. Meanwhile process the washed and dried parsley until finely chopped. Take out and reserve. Put the vegetables and stock into the bowl. (Unless you have one of the very big machines you will probably have to process the soup in two batches.) Switch on and process for 10 seconds, then check to see there are no big lumps of vegetables, but rather, a fine mince. Return to the saucepan, add the milk, and a little more water if the soup is of too thick a consistency. Heat through and serve in individual bowls, sprinkled thickly with the chopped parsley. Once again, crusty French bread is the ideal accompaniment.

TOMATO AND ORANGE

Tomato and orange began as a store cupboard soup, using ingredients like tins of tomatoes that were readily available in a crisis. Over the years it has become one of my favourite soups and certainly one of the most popular ones whenever I am cooking for a party. The ingredients to make it now have also changed to its enormous benefit. Passata and fresh orange juice are always available. It is still in some ways a larder soup in that you can almost always keep or find the ingredients for it in the larder without having to worry about buying them specially. Do trust me about the ingredients even though they seem unusual. To serve, float a slice of orange on top, sprinkled with parsley – it looks and tastes delicious.

Attachment
double-bladed knife

Ingredients
*¾ pint (½ litre) passata (smooth thick Italian tomato
purée sold in jars or tetrapacks – not concentrated
tomato purée)
1 medium onion
2 tablespoons polyunsaturated oil
½ pint (300 ml) freshly pressed orange juice (or long
life orange juice)
generous pinch of sugar
salt and pepper
To serve – 1 orange sliced thinly, 1 tablespoon
chopped parsley*

Method
Peel and chop the onion into very fine dice, fry in the oil until soft but not brown, add the passata (or tomato juice if you can't find passata) and the orange juice, the pinch of sugar and season generously. Simmer together for 25 minutes until thoroughly cooked through. Process until completely smooth with all the onion bits disappearing, check again for seasoning, pour into bowls, top with the orange and the parsley.
FOR PHOTOGRAPH TURN TO PAGE 15 (RIGHT)

CARROT SOUP

The lovely golden colour of this soup makes it extremely appetising, especially on a cold winter's day. The yoghurt is not traditional, but rather a modern, crafty touch – try it anyway, it cuts the sweetness of the carrots just perfectly for my taste.

Attachment
double-bladed knife

Ingredients
*1½ lb (675 g) carrots
2 medium sized potatoes
2 onions*

*1½ pints (900 ml) chicken stock
½ teaspoon turmeric
1 carton natural yoghurt
1–2 tablespoons oil
salt and pepper*

Method
Peel the vegetables and cut into chunks. Toss all the vegetables in a deep saucepan with a little oil to prevent them sticking, and sprinkle over the turmeric. Turn them until thoroughly coated. Add the chicken stock then bring to the boil and simmer on a medium heat for 25 minutes with a lid on the saucepan. Take out all the vegetables and enough stock to make a purée. Place in the bowl and process for 15 seconds. Return to the saucepan, season, heat through and pour into a tureen. Beat the pot of yoghurt until it's smooth and slightly runny, and stir it into the soup so that it swirls into a marble pattern.

In Eastern Europe they sometimes make a soup similar to this with a few caraway seeds added at the frying stage at the beginning. They make an interesting and unusual flavour alternative.
FOR PHOTOGRAPH TURN TO PAGE 15 (LEFT)

LENTIL SOUP

Rich warming lentil soups always seem to be a thing of legend or family reminiscence, but in fact they are one of the easiest in the world to make. And there is nothing more comforting and warming in the middle of a chill winter than a bowl of steaming lentil soup – fragrant with herbs, and really quite easy to prepare.

Attachment
double-bladed knife

Ingredients
*12 oz (350 g) red or green lentils
processor-chopped parsley and chives
2 pints (1200 ml) beef stock (water will do, but is not
so nice)
2 onions
2 carrots
1 teaspoon black treacle
1½ oz (30 g) butter
salt and pepper*

Method
Fry the lentils (which you have carefully made sure contain no small stones) in the butter, with the onions and carrots both peeled and cut into chunks. Turn until thoroughly coated with the butter then add the stock and simmer for 25 minutes for red lentils, or 35 for green. If all the liquid is being absorbed, add another half a pint of water. Pour half the mixture into the processor including all the large chunks of vegetables. Process until smooth; return to the pan; stir thoroughly and reheat. Season and serve with a little nob of butter and a sprinkling of parsley and chives in each bowl.

Fish soups are very poorly regarded in Britain. I don't know why, as we are surrounded by the sea, have terrific fish in our rivers and have always depended on fish as a major part of our staple diet. All over the rest of the world, from New England to Provence to Thailand fish soups are prized and enjoyed, but we have virtually no tradition of them at all except for a couple of Scottish recipes based on smoked haddock. What I have suggested here are two recipes which are both very economical and produce wonderful soups – the kind of which French gourmet restaurants are extremely proud. One is very southern in its styling and one northern. Both are scrumptious and shouldn't be missed. Do get your fishmonger to give you the cheap bits of fish to make them with – one of the pleasures of fish soups is that they are made from the bits that you get free when you have bought fish that has been filleted and cleaned for other dishes. Don't be afraid to ask for and cook the heads: they may not look too appetising but they produce a wonderful flavour and you really don't have to eat the bits you don't fancy.

MEDITERRANEAN FISH SOUP

Attachment
double-bladed knife

Ingredients
A couple of large fish heads and/or 1½ lb (675 g) of assorted fish trimmings
clove of garlic
1 large onion
1 lb (450 g) tin of tomatoes
1 bay leaf
2 tablespoons parsley
couple of sprigs of fennel (or teaspoon dried leaves)
3 tablespoons lemon juice
salt and pepper
To serve, four rounds of french bread that have been toasted crisp in the oven and a serving of garlic mayonnaise (page 35) into which you have stirred ½ teaspoon of tabasco.

Method
Wash the fish heads or fish trimmings, put them in a large saucepan and cover them generously with water. Bring them to the boil, skim off any froth and add the bayleaf, the parsley and the lemon juice, cover the whole lot and simmer for 40 minutes. Remove all the bits from the stock, put in a clove of garlic, the onion peeled and chopped roughly, the tomatoes with their juice and simmer for another 10 minutes with the vegetables in. Pour all of this into the processor and process for 15 seconds using bursts to make sure it is thoroughly blended. When the fish pieces have cooled take off any useful looking chunks of fish. You will be surprised how much is produced; throw the rest away and add half of the flesh that remains to the soup with the fennel and generous seasoning, process again for 5 seconds, pour into a bowl and add the remaining reserved pieces of fish to make the soup just a little bit chunky. To serve, float a slice of toasted bread on top of each bowl and add a spoonful of the garlic and chilli mayonnaise, stirring it into the soup.

FISH SOUP

This is a more northern soup with an almost Scandinavian flavour which derives from the dill in it. You can buy dill fresh from many supermarkets now, or dried if you can't get the fresh kind. Either way it's pretty crucial to the flavour of the soup so try and find it if you can. You can, of course, grow it in your own garden; it is a very easy-to-grow annual.

Attachment
double-bladed knife

Ingredients
1 lb (450 g) fish trimmings
8 oz (675 g) fish fillet, haddock, cod or coley
1 large onion
2 tablespoons fresh, 1 tablespoon dried dill
2 stalks celery
½ pint (300 ml) milk
1 dessertspoon cornflour
salt and pepper

Method
Put the fish trimmings, not the fillet, into a saucepan, cover with a pint (600 ml) of water and simmer for 20 minutes. Discard the trimmings and to the stock add the onion, the dill, the celery and the milk; simmer for another 10 minutes and put into the processor with cornflour and seasoning. Process until smooth, return to the heat and cook until the cornflour thickens the soup. This should take about 2 minutes. Cut the white fish, which should be thoroughly free of bones and skin, into ½ inch dice, add it to the soup, simmer for 5 minutes, check the seasoning and serve.

CHUNKY CHICKEN CHOWDER

This is the ideal dish to make if you have the remains of a chicken. It's another 'meal in a bowl', similar in some ways to the American chowders that have become almost legendary because of their savoury richness.

Attachment
double-bladed knife

Ingredients
1 raw chicken carcass
2 pints (1200 ml) water
bay leaf
celery stalk
head of parsley
1 large onion
small packet frozen mixed vegetables
1 egg
1 teaspoon cornflour
salt and pepper

Method
Cover the carcass with water, bring to the boil, skim off any froth. Add the herbs and celery; cover and simmer for 1 hour. Remove the bones and chicken meat from the liquid and pour the stock into the bowl. Switch on, add the cornflour mixed with a little cold water and the egg. Process until smooth, return to the pan; cook over a gentle heat until the mixture thickens, just below the boil. Add the onion, chopped finely (you can do this in the processor bowl without washing it out again) and the packet of frozen mixed vegetables which do not need to be defrosted or cooked. Simmer for just 5 minutes. Remove any good meat from the chicken carcass. Cut it into chunks; add it to the soup; and serve, well seasoned, in a large tureen.

FRENCH ONION SOUP

This recipe is always preceded in cookery books with tales of how the writer first had it early one morning in Les Halles, the famous fruit and vege-table market in Paris. Unfortunately, by the time I got there they were pulling Les Halles down, but I've managed to eat it in a number of French restaurants both in France and throughout the world, and I can verify the genuine Gallic taste in this version. And you don't have to be up at 6 a.m. to taste it!

Attachments
slicing disc
grating disc

Ingredients
2 lb (900 g) onions
1 oz (25 g) beef dripping
1 teaspoon sugar
2 pints (1200 ml) beef stock
1 dessertspoon Worcester sauce
1/2 French loaf
4 oz (100 g) cheese (Gruyère is perfect, Gouda is fine)
salt and pepper

Method
Peel and halve the onions and put them through the slicing disc. Melt the dripping and fry the onions mixed with the teaspoon of sugar until they are brown but not burnt. This should take about 5 minutes over a medium heat. The sugar will help to caramelise them and produce the rich dark flavour and colour characteristic of this soup. Add the Worcester sauce and a seasoning of salt and pepper; pour over the stock and simmer very gently for at least 35 minutes, stirring occasionally. The onions should almost melt into the soup, but still have a slight texture of their own. Cut the French bread into 1/2 inch slices and put these to toast in a low oven, while you grate the cheese into a clean, dry bowl. To serve the soup, put a ladleful into each fire-proof dish, float a piece of the toast on the top, and heap some grated cheese on top of that. Cook under the grill for just a minute until the cheese is melted, and serve bubbling hot, being careful not to eat it too quickly lest you singe your tongue in your enthusiasm.

OPPOSITE: CHUNKY CHICKEN CHOWDER IS A 'MEAL IN A BOWL'. SERVED WITH FRENCH BREAD.

GAZPACHO

This is an unusual soup from the Andalusian region of Spain. There are a number of different versions of it, ranging from a thin, garlicky liquid with a few bits and pieces floating around in it, to a full scale salad which couldn't be called a soup with the best will in the world. This is one of my favourites to serve on a hot summer's day, especially at a weekend buffet party. If you are a bit nervous about the garlic, you can cut down on it, but try not to leave it out altogether. My version falls somewhere between the extremes of the do-it-yourself-dinner-party Gazpacho and the thin-as-dish-water Gazpacho, both of which have their supporters.

Attachments
grating disc
double-bladed knife

Ingredients
1 cucumber
1 Spanish onion
8 oz (225 g) tomatoes
1 clove garlic
1 small green pepper
2 × 1 inch (2.5 cm) slices wholemeal bread
2 tablespoons each, lemon juice and olive oil
20 oz (550 ml) tin tomato juice
½ pint (300 ml) water
salt and pepper

Method
Grate the unpeeled cucumber. Empty the bowl (there is no need to wash it), put in the knife. Add the quartered onion and the garlic and process until finely chopped. Add the quartered tomatoes and cleaned green pepper and process again for 2 seconds. Add half the tomato juice, the oil and the lemon juice and process for 5 seconds. Pour into a bowl, stir in the remaining tomato juice, the water and the cucumber. Season quite strongly with salt and pepper, and a pinch of sugar if the soup lacks sweetness from the tomatoes. Cut the bread into 1 inch cubes and place in a bowl on the table. Chill the soup in the fridge for at least an hour, and before serving add a couple of ice cubes per person. To serve it, ladle it into bowls and add the brown bread cubes individually to people's choice. A little grated cucumber and chopped onion and tomato mixture, kept separately in small bowls, can be added at the table if you choose, and is really quite *olé!*

VICHYSSOISE

This is a cold soup made from very ordinary ingredients like leeks and potatoes, but when properly blended and served with a swirl of ice cold cream it is one of the great haute cuisine dishes of restaurants around the world. It's supposed to have been developed in America, when a French chef, who'd made it as a hot soup, was kept waiting so long by an insensitive guest he let the soup get cold and added the cream as a last minute guilty thought. Whether that story is true or not, it's certainly worth your while trying it without any guilt whatsoever.

Attachment
double-bladed knife

Ingredients
1½ lb (675 g) potatoes
1½ lb (675 g) leeks
1 onion
2 tablespoons oil
1½ pints (900 ml) chicken stock
4 oz (100 g) double cream
salt and pepper

Method
Peel the potatoes and onion and cut into 1 inch sized cubes. Peel the broken leaves off the leeks. Slice them in half lengthwise and leave in cold water for at least 10 minutes before washing thoroughly to clear all the dirt out. Cut into 1 inch lengths and fry gently, with the onion and potatoes, in oil for 5 minutes or until all the vegetables are softened. Add a good pinch of salt and pepper, cover with the stock and simmer for 30 minutes. The vegetables should be completely soft but not disintegrated. Add all the vegetables and enough stock to let the blades work, to the bowl. Process until the vegetables are completely smooth, adding a little more stock if necessary as they blend. Return the mixture to the remaining stock in the saucepan and stir until completely smooth. Pour into a bowl and chill in the refrigerator for at least 2 hours until thoroughly cold. To serve, ladle the soup into individual bowls, swirl the double cream around the top so it forms a spiral, and sprinkle the top of the soup with some freshly chopped green chives. If there aren't any available use the freeze-dried version instead. Serve it with hot French bread, lashings of butter and bags of confidence.

These are variations on vegetable soups. Following the method of making *potage bonne femme*, here are some of my favourite variations for making other kinds of vegetable soups. The technique is basically the same, preparing the vegetables, cutting them up and frying them in a little oil and/or butter, adding the water or stock, cooking and then processing.

Courgette Soup

This is ideal in the summer when courgettes are both cheap and plentiful. It is a beautiful pale green soup that processes quite coarsely and can be eaten hot, or puréed really finely. With a little cream, it makes a wonderful cold soup.

Attachment
double-bladed knife

Ingredients
*1 lb (450 g) courgettes topped and tailed
1 large onion
1 pint (600 ml) water
½ pint (300 ml) milk (this can be semi-skimmed)
1 medium sized potato, peeled
2 tablespoons oil*

Method
Fry the vegetables in the oil having cut them all into ½-inch pieces. Add the liquids and simmer for 20 minutes, season and process.

Pumpkin and Tomato Soup

This is a favourite from the Mediterranean region but pumpkins are very widely available in the autumn in Britain now and make a wonderful golden coloured soup. This one, I think, is best only lightly processed so that there is still some texture left to both the onion and the tomatoes. The pumpkin, once it is cooked, will go to a smooth purée at the touch of the processor blade.

Attachment
Double-bladed knife

Ingredients
*8 oz (225 g) pumpkin peeled and cubed
8 oz (225 g) onion peeled
8 oz (225 g) fresh tomatoes
½ teaspoon thyme
½ teaspon basil
1½ pints (900 ml) chicken stock (or water)
2 tablespoons sunflower or polyunsaturated oil
salt and pepper*

Method
Cut the onion and tomatoes into walnut size pieces. Fry gently in the oil for 5 minutes with the pumpkin. Add the stock or water, season generously, add the herbs, and simmer for 25 minutes until the pumpkin is soft. Process in 1- or 2-second bursts, leaving the pumpkin and stock as a smooth base with the onion and tomatoes still providing some texture. Serve hot. Croutons go very well with this.

Celery, Stilton and Apple Soup

An unusual and rather rural English soup with a very satisfying flavour, particularly nice on cold days.

Attachment
double-bladed knife

Ingredients
*1 head celery, trimmed
2 cooking apples approximately 1 lb (450 g) to 1½ lb (675 g) in weight
1 large onion
4 oz (100 g) Stilton
salt and pepper
2 pints (1200 ml) water*

Method
Peel and quarter the onion. Fry gently in oil. Slice the celery across the stalk into ½-inch pieces and add. Quarter, core and add the apples. Turn gently, season, add the water and cook for 25 minutes until the apples have disintegrated into pulp. Put the soup into the food processor and blend until well puréed. Add half the cheese and process again for 5 seconds. Serve with the remaining cheese crumbled over each serving. A couple of celery leaves on the top with the final crumbling of Stilton makes the soup look especially attractive.

Pâtés and Potted Meats

Pâtés have had a bad press recently. There have been a lot of scares and fears, particularly about the imported ones that sit for days on the delicatessen counters of supermarkets before you buy your slice. With a food processor all that is unnecessary – both the buying of the slice and the worrying about it afterwards. Pâtés used to be hard work. I can remember mincing and mincing again the ingredients, scraping out the blades of the mincer, mixing and blending, at least a morning's work for a couple of good sized pâtés. All that has been a thing of the past for years now, because of my food processor. In fact, I don't make large pâtés any more unless I am having a big party. I make small ones because they are so easy to make, the only time really taken is that of allowing them to mature in the fridge. What's more, the texture I get is usually far better than I ever managed with a mincer and at least as good as that which you get with the professionally made pâtés. I have suggested a range of pâtés from the very simple to the special, from smoked mackerel right the way through to a rather grand duck pâté suitable for very fine occasions or grand buffet parties. I have

also included a couple of nouvelle cuisine style fish terrines. These are often thought to be very difficult to make and recipes often include chilling bowls, placing them in crushed ice, and hand-mincing ingredients – all of which is totally unnecessary if you have a good processor.

There are also a number of recipes for potted meats, fish and cheese. Potting is the English equivalent of the European pâté tradition, developed over centuries in Britain, with its high point in the Edwardian period. Potted meats and fish make wonderful first courses. They have the advantage that they can be served in individual pots or pretty little dishes, a thing you can't do very easily with pâtés, and they also allow you to use up left-overs in a very special way – you can use anything – beef, salmon, or even bits of cheese. You can also adapt your favourite recipes, or vary the ingredients, perhaps adding a little game liver to the chicken liver pâté or substituting some wonderful plump fresh kippers for the smoked mackerel. In any case, you are in for the sort of treat that no delicatessen can offer you, and with none of the worries.

Posh Chicken Liver Pâté

This one is for a special occasion when a little light starter is just what's called for.

Attachment
double-bladed knife

Ingredients
8 oz (225 g) chicken livers
3 oz (75 g) butter
2 eggs
liqueur glass apple juice
salt and pepper

Method
Defrost and drain the chicken livers. Melt 2 oz (50 g) butter in a thick sided pan and turn the livers in the melted, foaming butter for about 2 minutes, until they're brown on the outside but not hard. Put them into the bowl. Add the remaining butter to the pan, and in it scramble the 2 eggs until they are firm; add them and the small glass of apple juice to the bowl, season generously and process the whole mixture for 10 seconds. Scrape down the sides of the bowl and process for another 10 seconds until thoroughly mixed and very fine. Pour it into a white sided soufflé dish. Melt a little more butter in the pan and pour it over, running it carefully around the top to seal. Place the soufflé dish in the fridge for at least 2 hours to set before serving. This is particularly nice with hot buttered toast, for it has a lovely soft, delicate spreading consistency.

Rustic Chicken Liver Pâté

A pâté strictly to be eaten by those with a taste for strong, delicious country-type foods.

Attachment
double-bladed knife

Ingredients
3 oz (75 g) chicken livers
4 oz (100 g) chicken hearts
4 oz (100 g) butter
2 cloves garlic
juice and rind of an orange
1 teaspoon dried thyme
1 teaspoon dried tarragon
salt and pepper

Method
Poach the chicken hearts (most butchers will supply these or you can use all chicken livers) in a small saucepan, generously covered with water, for 30 minutes. Remove, drain, trim off any gristly bits. Cut each heart in half, place in the bowl with the double-bladed knife. In the drained pan, melt all but $\frac{1}{2}$ oz (13 g) of the butter until foaming. Add the chicken livers and garlic, and brown the livers until they are cooked but still slightly pink in the middle (test one to check). Add these to the bowl and rinse out the pan with the orange juice. Add that to the bowl with the grated orange rind, the herbs and seasonings. Cover and process for 20 seconds. Scrape down the sides, process again for another 10 seconds. The mixture should still have a little texture, be a bit grainy from the tiny bits of heart in the mixture. Pack it into an oval, earthenware dish and melt the last remaining butter to pour round the top as a seal. Leave it in the fridge, overnight if you can, for the flavours to blend. You can slice this pâté, or scoop it out of the bowl with a spoon. Either way, the centre of it should still be a little pink, and the flavour of the garlic and herbs should have blended thoroughly into the chicken livers.

Pâtés and Potted Meats

COUNTRY PÂTÉ

This is perhaps the most basic and simple of all pâtés, the kind that in restaurants is usually called 'Pâté du Chef'. That is unless the chef happens to be a master or a show off, in which case I refer you to Duck en Croûte which is coming up in a little while. But this is basically a liver pâté. It's flavoured with herbs and designed to be spread in large chunks on crusty bread. If you're putting a picnic together, take some with you, still in its terrine and use a spoon to serve it onto the bread when you get to the picnic site. A good grainy French mustard goes extremely well with this pâté, or a few dill-flavoured gherkins make a nice sharp contrast to its richness.

Attachment
double-bladed knife

Ingredients
1 lb (450 g) lambs liver
4 oz (100 g) beef kidney fat or suet
2 × 1 inch (2.5 cm) slices of bread
1 large onion
1 teaspoon thyme
1 teaspoon oregano
2 eggs
2 bay leaves
salt and pepper

Method
Make breadcrumbs with the bread broken into pieces, and add the peeled, quartered onion. Process until puréed (about 10 seconds). Take it out and put aside. Into the bowl put the liver and the beef fat, both cut into 1 inch cubes. Process for 20 seconds. Scrape down the sides, add the thyme and oregano, a generous amount of salt and pepper, and the eggs, one at a time, while the motor is running. Switch off and add the bread and onion mixture. Process until thoroughly mixed. Pack into an oval terrine which will fit inside a baking dish and place the bay leaves on top. Fill the baking dish with water an inch deep, place the terrine in it and put the whole lot in an oven, 350°F, 180°C, gas mark 4 for 1¼ hours. You can if you like cover the top of the pâté with a sheet of foil placed lightly over it. When it's cooked and the sides have shrunk away from the terrine a little, take it out, and allow it to cool for at least 12 hours, weighted down with a plate and a couple of 1 lb or 2 lb tins from the larder. When it's cool it'll keep in the fridge with a layer of cling-film around it for over a week, or for 4 days once it's been cut.

SMOKED MACKEREL PÂTÉ

Smoked mackerel are one of the great crafty gourmet delicacies – still about the cheapest fish we have, and yet tasting as fine, or finer, to my mind, than smoked salmon. When you are making this pâté, which has become a firm favourite in restaurants throughout the country in recent years, try and choose mackerel that are not too brightly coloured but have been turned a golden brown by smoke and not bright yellow by chemical dyes. There are even some fishmongers these days who are smoking their own. Also on the market are Scandinavian-style home smokers, about the size of a shoe box, which produce quite the most delicious smoked fish I have ever tasted in my life.

Attachment
double-bladed knife

Ingredients
8 oz (225 g) smoked mackerel (fillets are fine)
4 oz (100 g) cream cheese (either fresh or Philadelphia style, or fromage frais for a low-fat version)
2 oz (50 g) butter
¼ teaspoon nutmeg
½ teaspoon freshly ground black pepper
1 lemon
salt and pepper

Method
Skin and carefully bone the mackerel fillets, place them in the bowl with the cream cheese, the juice of half the lemon, the spices and seasonings. Process for 10 seconds, scrape down the bowl and process again until the mixture is thoroughly smooth and blended. Melt the butter, and with the motor running add half of it to the mixture. Switch off and pack it into attractive serving dishes. It can either be in individual ramekins for individual servings, or in a big soufflé dish for the centre of the table. Slice the other half lemon into very thin complete slices, removing any pips, and lay these in an overlapping pattern around the top of the pâté (or put a single lemon slice on each ramekin). Pour the remaining melted butter over the top to seal it, and set in the fridge for at least 2 hours before serving.

Very thin brown bread and butter is traditional with this, but I must admit that hot, oven-fresh French bread is my favourite.

DUCK PÂTÉ

Traditionally duck pâtés are rich, grand and for special occasions. They are also, by many of today's standards, too rich in fat to be healthy or even sensible eating. They are undoubtedly delicious. The richness of duck makes a particularly good, attractive and succulent pâté so I have modified some earlier ideas and produced what I hope is light and delicate with a strong orange flavour. Use a non-stick loaf tin if you have one, it makes both the turning out and the washing up a great deal easier and also makes keeping the pâté in the fridge to mature much safer. To serve, slice like a loaf in half-inch slices with a very sharp knife. Lay these on large plates with perhaps a little oak leaf lettuce salad with a walnut oil dressing and a slice or two of very carefully skinned orange to add to the bite and prettiness.

Attachment
double-bladed knife

Ingredients
1 roast duck (approx. 4¹/₂ lb, 2 kg)
1 orange and 1 lemon both preferably unwaxed
1 clove garlic
1 inch (2.5 cm) root ginger, peeled
2 tablespoons soy sauce
1 teaspoon salt
2 eggs
1 teaspoon dried thyme

1 **Place the prepared orange into bowl. Process until well chopped. Add the garlic and ginger and process until mixed together.**

Method
Place the duck on a roasting rack over a roasting pan and bake in a hot oven, 400°F, 200°C, gas mark 6, for 1 hour 10 minutes. Wash the orange and lemon thoroughly, cut into quarters and remove all seeds and stalks, cut into ¹/₄ inch slices, place in the processor and blend until well chopped. Add the peeled garlic and the ginger cut into chunks, process again until thoroughly mixed together. When the duck is cooked remove it from the oven and allow it to cool. Take off the skin and set aside, remove the flesh from the bones, keeping one of the breasts as intact as possible, put the rest into the processor with all the other ingredients, process until the meat is well chopped but not totally puréed. Butter a 2 lb (900 g) non-stick loaf tin and line with butter papers which will make for easy removal. Put half the chopped mixture into the tin, slice the remaining whole breast into narrow slices and lay those carefully overlapping along the length of the mixture, cover with the other half of the mixture, fold the butter papers over, tap the tin to settle the mixture and place it in a baking tin in which you have an inch of water. Place the baking tin in an oven, 350°F, 180°C, gas mark 4 for 45–50 minutes. Remove the pâté from the water jacket, allow to cool and cover with cling film. It can be eaten as soon as it is cool but is much better after three days in the refrigerator after it has matured and the flavours blended. It is delicious eaten with a fruity mango or exotic fruit chutney.

2 **Add the meat from the cooked duck, reserving one breast, and process until chopped. Place half the mixture into a lined tin.**

3 Cut the remaining whole breast into narrow slices.

4 Lay the slices, carefully overlapping, along the length of the mixture. Cover with remaining mixture. Fold the paper over the top.

SERVE DUCK PÂTÉ WITH A GARNISH OF ORANGE SLICES AND PARSLEY

Fish terrines have become the darlings of the nouvelle cuisine set. I have a suspicion about nouvelle cuisine which is that it is a method of charging main course prices for starters, but certainly a really good, delicate and delicious fish terrine is one of the highlights of nouvelle cuisine cooking. It is easy to achieve now in your own home despite the terribly complicated instructions you can sometimes get for making them. If you would like an easy recipe, there are two here, one plain and one fancy, both delicious. The real difference is in the expense of the ingredients and the exotic presentation. When you are cutting them make sure they are really well chilled and you are using a very sharp knife. A fish slice to help move the pieces onto plates so that they remain in perfect condition is a pretty good idea as well.

SALMON AND MONKFISH

This is the fancy version which you can produce at the grandest occasion and feel totally confident about. The ingredients can be varied according to what's available. What I have suggested here produces a three-colour terrine, rather like one of those Neapolitan icecreams from my youth.

Attachment
double-bladed knife

Ingredients
8 oz (225 g) fresh salmon, skinned and boned
8 oz (225 g) monkfish, skinned and boned
8 oz (225 g) whiting fillets, skinned
4 oz (100 g) stringless French beans
4 oz (100 g) baby carrots
1 oz (25 g) fresh dill and/or parsley with 1 teaspoon dried dill
3 eggs
6 oz (175 g) fromage frais
2 tablespoons oil
1 teaspoon salt
lemon juice

Method
Cut all the fish into 1 inch cubes, keeping the different kinds separate. Place the salmon in the processor with 1 egg, 2 oz (50 g) of fromage frais and ½ tablespoon oil, process until smooth and place in a non-stick 2 lb (900 g) loaf tin which you have carefully oiled and lined with butter or greaseproof paper. Peel the carrots and blanch them in boiling water for 4 minutes, adding the topped and tailed beans, and blanch for 1 more minute. Drain, and rinse in cold water. Halve the carrots and put a layer of carrot over the salmon mixture. Into the food processor put the monkfish, one egg, 2 oz (50 g) fromage frais, another ½ tablespoon oil, half the salt and 1 tablespoon lemon juice, process until smooth and cover the carrots with the mixture. Put the beans on top of the monkfish, rinse the bowl and blade, put in the whiting fillets, the remaining egg and 2 oz (50 g) fromage frais, the remaining oil, the herbs and remaining salt and process thoroughly until smooth. Pour this over the beans, tap the tin to settle carefully and place the whole lot in a baking tin with an inch of water in it. Cover the top with butter or grease-proof paper and bake for 45 minutes at 350°F, 180°C, gas mark 4. The pâté will shrink away from the tin a little. Take it from the baking tin, allow to cool for half an hour and chill thoroughly in the fridge before turning out, removing the butter papers and slicing for serving.

FOR PHOTOGRAPH TURN TO PAGE 25

HADDOCK AND EGG

While no less delicious than its colleague, this is much simpler to make and absolutely wonderful for family meals or parties. It has a delicate flavour and rich texture that make it a favourite with everyone.

Attachment
double-bladed knife

Ingredients
1½ lb (675 g) haddock fillets, skinned and boned
2 hard boiled eggs
1 tablespoon parsley
1 tablespoon chives
3 eggs
2 tablespoons oil (not olive)
½ teaspoon salt
juice and rind of 1 lemon

Method
Cut the fish into 1 inch cubes, add the oil, fresh eggs, lemon juice and salt, and process until smooth. Pour into a bowl leaving approximately a breakfast cup full in the processor. Add the shelled, halved hard boiled eggs, the herbs and the rind of the lemon, and process briefly until roughly chopped. Line a 2 inch, non-stick oiled loaf tin with greaseproof or buttered paper. Add the layers, starting with half the plain mixture, followed by the eggs and herbs, smooth, then add the remaining plain mixture. Cover the top with greaseproof or buttered paper and bake in a water-filled baking dish for 45 minutes at 350°F, 180°C, gas mark 4, or until a skewer pushed into the terrine comes out clean. Allow to cool and then chill, preferably overnight, before slicing into ¾ inch slices to serve. This is particularly nice with one of the herb-flavoured mayonnaises you will find on page 35.

Note
This terrine can be made with very lightly smoked haddock instead of the fresh, or a mixture of the two.

POTTED TURKEY

Perfect for post-Christmas use of the inevitable turkey bits – the scraps that you otherwise can't find a use for go perfectly into this dish. As most people will have had their fill of turkey by the time you get round to making this, why not cover it when it's made, and put it in the freezer. A couple of months later it may prove a revelation which excites praise and smiles instead of groans and head-holding, which it might do the day after Boxing Day.

Attachment
double-bladed knife

Ingredients
8 oz (225 g) turkey scraps (even skin will do, though it shouldn't be exclusively skin)
2 or 3 tablespoons giblet stock or gravy
4 oz (100 g) butter
½ teaspoon salt
½ teaspoon black pepper
couple of tablespoons cranberry sauce (if available)
slice white bread or 2 tablespoons stuffing

Method
Put the bread or stuffing into the bowl, process for 2 or 3 seconds until crumbed. Add the turkey scraps, all the spices and flavourings except the butter and process until a fine purée, scraping down the sides. If you haven't stock or gravy, use water because turkey is very dry. The processing should take about 15 seconds. Melt the butter and add it, with the motor running, through the feed-tube until the whole mixture is thoroughly blended. Pot in individual bowls, or in a bigger soufflé dish for general use. If serving fairly soon a small teaspoon of cranberry sauce piled in the middle with a couple of sprigs of holly makes an attractive decoration. Don't freeze it with the holly on though, it won't taste nice, and it'll make holes in the cling film!

FOR PHOTOGRAPH TURN TO PAGE 32 (RIGHT)

POTTED CHEESE

Potted cheese is in fact a very old English tradition, deriving I'm sure, from our having hard cheeses which often leave dried out remnants. These are only fit for grating, so the Continent, with its softer cheeses has never actually discovered the pleasure of this particular recipe. There's an exotic ingredient in this one as well, the mango chutney, which comes from one of Britain's other traditions – that of involving Eastern foods and flavours in its national cooking. Anyone who's ever tried a cheese and chutney sandwich and enjoyed it, is going to find this particular savoury especially succulent.

Attachments
grating disc
double-bladed knife

Ingredients
8 oz (225 g) English cheese; Cheddar, Wensleydale, Double Gloucester or Cheshire are best (it can be old and dried)
4 oz (100 g) butter
2 tablespoons mango chutney
1 teaspoon lemon juice
½ teaspoon black pepper
pinch cayenne pepper

Method
Grate the cheese into the bowl and, without emptying, replace the grating disc with the double-bladed mixing knife. Add the lemon juice, chutney and spices and the butter, softened to room temperature but not melted, and process for 10 seconds, scrape down the sides and process again. Taste – it may need a little salt if the cheese was particularly mild. You can serve this, either in ramekins like the other potted meats, or, equally attractively piled up on a pretty plate and shaped with the prongs of a fork, so that it looks rather like an old fashioned butter pat. Both its texture and taste will surprise people. And in the unlikely event of you being lucky enough to have any left over, it makes a wonderful Welsh Rarebit, melted on toast under the grill next day.

FOR PHOTOGRAPH TURN TO PAGE 32 (LEFT)

POTTED TONGUE

If you ever cook tongues yourself and slice them, hot or cold, you may find yourself with bits left over. These are perfect for this recipe, as are scraps left from shop-bought tongues, or even a 'quarter' bought specially for the purpose. There's a very meaty flavour to this recipe, and it goes especially well with old fashioned English-type chutneys, or mustard a little stronger than the French care for.

Attachment
double-bladed knife

Ingredients
4 oz (100 g) cooked tongue
4 oz (100 g) unsalted or mildly salted butter
½ teaspoon each, black pepper and mustard powder
1 dessertspoon redcurrant jelly
generous pinch ground allspice

Method
Place all the ingredients except the butter in the bowl (you can cut the tongue up if it's in large chunks), and process briefly (about 10 seconds). Melt the butter, start the motor again and pour the melted, foaming not-browned butter through the feed-tube until the mixture is thoroughly blended. Do not add any salt. The tongue, and possibly even the butter, have more than enough salt in them already. Scrape out the bowl carefully and pack the potted meat into individual ramekins or small dishes. Let it set (it doesn't have to be in the fridge). It will keep, covered, for nearly a week.

POTTED MEAT AND CHEESE MAKE WONDERFUL FIRST COURSES. FROM LEFT TO RIGHT: CHEESE, TONGUE AND TURKEY

Dressings and Sauces

Some of the nicest things about French cooking are the sauces. They almost never come out of bottles, although occasionally something that comes out of bottles goes into them. Rather, they are a blend of simple ingredients mixed with great care and skill to produce sumptuous and smooth coatings and glazes for the food. The marvellous thing about processors is that they have that skill and care, so all you need are the simple ingredients and a little time. Don't be afraid to experiment with the sauces. In Britain our classic cauliflower with cheese sauce, or, if you're from the North, leeks with white sauce, seems to be about our limit. But, in France, you might get carrots in a *béchamel* sauce flavoured with caraway seeds, broad beans in a rich parsley sauce, or hard-boiled eggs covered in a creamy onion sauce and browned under the grill. Enjoy yourself – the world of super sauces is at your finger tips, and you don't need much more time to make them than read about them.

In Britain, only too often, we tend to regard salad cream as the be all and end all of salad dressings. While I have nothing against salad cream, I do think there are a lot of rather more exciting things to put on your lettuce. Here are some rather unusual ideas for dressings that could probably go on most lettuce, cucumber, beetroot and tomato salads without have to explore the realms of exotic ingredients. You can find ideas for salads on pages 41-46.

LEMON DRESSING

This is my version of what's known variously as *vinaigrette* or French dressing. It's a flavour combination that comes from the Middle East where there is an enormous variety of salads. The lemon juice is lighter than vinegar in similar recipes, and has the other great advantage of not destroying any flavours in the foods you might be eating the salad with.

Attachment
double-bladed knife

Ingredients
$\frac{1}{2}$ cup salad oil
$\frac{1}{4}$ cup lemon juice (fresh, or bottled is fine)
$\frac{1}{2}$ teaspoon mustard powder
$\frac{1}{2}$ teaspoon salt
1 teaspoon sugar

Method
Put all the ingredients, except the oil, into the bowl and process for 3 to 5 seconds. Take out the plastic pusher and pour in the oil in a steady stream. The dressing will thicken quite dramatically and to a lovely single-cream consistency.

A variation on this dressing which is becoming increasingly popular abroad, but very rarely tried here, is garlic and herbs. You will need 2 peeled and quartered cloves of garlic and a handful of herbs (parsley, basil and watercress seem to be the favourites), finely chopped. Then add the lemon juice and seasonings and proceed as above.

LIME DRESSING

If you can find them, use the large green Persian limes for this one.

Attachment
double-bladed knife

Ingredients
$\frac{1}{2}$ cup salad oil
juice of 2 limes – squeezed
$\frac{1}{2}$ teaspoon salt
1 teaspoon soft brown sugar

Method
Put all the ingredients except the oil into the bowl, process for 3 to 5 seconds; while processing pour in the oil at a steady stream and stop processing as soon as the dressing thickens. This is particularly nice used with tropical ingredients or shell fish, avocados, star fruit or big babacowa fruit, grown in the Channel Islands under glass. Prawns, shrimps, flaked white fish or monkfish go beautifully with lime dressing.

MALTAISE ORANGE DRESSING

Substitute the juice of a blood orange for half the lemon juice to produce a very pretty bright pink dressing.

BLUE CHEESE

This is an American dressing, made in expensive restaurants by a head waiter mashing the cheese with a silver fork. It may look good, but doesn't taste anything like as good as the processor product. No silver fork wielded by a Maitre d'. ever managed the blend of smoothness and sharpness achieved by your friendly electric chef.

Attachment
double-bladed knife

Ingredients
6 oz (175 g) blue cheese
coffee cup of milk
$\frac{1}{2}$ teaspoon made mustard
$\frac{1}{4}$ pint (150 ml) oil
$\frac{1}{2}$ teaspoon granulated sugar
1 tablespoon lemon juice

Method
Crumble the blue cheese roughly and add it with the milk to the bowl and process for about 5 seconds. Scrape down the sides and add mustard, sugar and the lemon juice if you like your dressings really sharp. Put the lid on, switch on, remove the plastic pusher and pour in the oil in a slight steady stream. It should never go in all at once, but be added gradually. As the oil is added you will notice a change in the noise of the motor and the blades will slow down suddenly as the dressing becomes thick. The more oil you add, the thicker it becomes. I like it just this side of softly whipped double cream. Try it with your regular salads, or with quarters of American Iceberg or Webbs Wonder style lettuce, washed but left whole in the head. Almost a meal in itself.

1 **Press together all the ingredients except the oil. Add a quarter of the oil and process again.**

2 **With the engine running, gradually add the remaining oil.**

MAYONNAISE

Said to have been invented in honour of one of Napoleon's victories, the history of this sauce goes back a lot further than the early nineteenth century. Traditionally one of the most difficult sauces of all to make – with oil being added drop by drop, the egg yolks being beaten by hand with a wooden spoon – it is now, thanks to electricity, one of the easiest and quickest to make at home. Have courage, and if it does go wrong, and curdles by some accident or mistake, simply pour it out of the bowl, add another egg, and gradually add the curdled mixture – you'll just have twice as much mayonnaise at the end.

Attachment
double-bladed knife

Ingredients
1 whole egg
½ teaspoon salt
½ teaspoon granulated sugar
2 teaspoons lemon juice
½ teaspoon made French mustard
8 fl oz (250 ml) salad oil

Method
Put the egg, mustard, salt, sugar and lemon juice into a bowl. Cover and process for 10 seconds. Add a quarter of the oil and process for another 5 seconds. Remove the plastic pusher and pour in the rest of the oil gradually with the engine running, in a slow, steady stream. The engine note will suddenly change as the mayonnaise thickens. You can go on adding oil with the mayonnaise getting thicker as you go.

You can double the quantities if you wish and you may find you have to if you own one of the big capacity processors. The mayonnaise, which has a lovely light lemony flavour, will keep perfectly well in reasonably large quantities in the fridge if well covered.

GREEN MAYONNAISE

A variation is to blend a generous handful of green herbs – parsley, young spinach leaves, chives or a little sorrel are the favourite candidates. Process for 10 seconds before the mayonnaise is made and put aside. Once the mayonnaise has thickened, stop the motor, add the herbs, scrape down the sides, switch on again, adding a little more oil, and turn out your *mayonnaise* or *sauce verte* which is used not only as a salad dressing but as a delicious accompaniment to cold beef or tongue.

BÉCHAMEL OR WHITE SAUCE

This is the basic sauce of French cooking. It's one of those sauces that, if it's right, is absolutely delicious, and if it's wrong, is a lumpy nightmare. It's the basis of some of the most delicious dishes in the world – and with a processor will work every time.

Attachment
double-bladed knife

Ingredients
1¹/₂ tablespoons softened butter
1¹/₂ tablespoons flour
¹/₂ pint (300 ml) milk
pinch salt
pinch ground nutmeg

Method
Make sure the butter is soft, almost to the point of being runny. Add the butter, flour, salt and nutmeg to the bowl; pour in the milk and process for 10 seconds. Tip the whole mixture into a saucepan (non-stick is best, it helps with the washing up and you don't waste any of the sauce). Stir over a medium heat until the sauce thickens and goes shiny. Turn the heat down and allow to simmer 4 or 5 minutes to make sure the flour is all cooked through. This is basic *béchamel* or white sauce.

SAUCE MORNAY

Put 6 oz (175 g) of cheese through the grating disc and after the sauce has cooked for 4 minutes, stir it in over a low heat. When melted, stir again and allow to settle for 1 minute over the lowest possible heat. This the French call *sauce mornay*, and is delicious used on fish, but will ennoble even one of our humble cauliflowers.

SAUCE SOUBISE (ONION SAUCE)

Cook a finely sliced onion in half a tablespoonful of butter until it's soft but not coloured. After making the *béchamel* stir the onion in and simmer very slowly for 5 minutes to allow the flavours to become infused. *Sauce soubise* is delicious with sausages, or poured over hard-boiled eggs and glazed under the grill.

PARSLEY SAUCE

For a classic English parsley sauce, process a good handful of parsley heads and broad stalks for 5 seconds, scrape the sides down and process for another 5 seconds or until super finely chopped. Scrape out into a bowl and keep. Make the *béchamel*, and just before serving add the chopped parsley and a squeeze of lemon juice.

1 **Place the soft butter, flour, salt and nutmeg into the bowl**

2 **Pour in the milk and process for 10 seconds**

3 Tip the mixture into a saucepan.

4 Stir over a medium heat, until the sauce thickens and goes shiny. Simmer for 4 or 5 minutes.

LUMPY SAUCES ARE AN IMPOSSIBILITY WITH A PROCESSOR. FROM LEFT TO RIGHT: BÉCHAMEL, MORNAY, PARSLEY, SOUBISE

Sauce Béarnaise

This is the French sauce for red meats. It's supposed to have been James Bond's favourite with steak. Certainly *Chateaubriand* with *sauce béarnaise* is one of the classic dishes of haute cuisine. But, if you're feeling the pinch a bit towards the end of the week, it's quite nice with hamburgers too. It's amazing what a transformation a little special touch like that can make to an everyday family meal.

Attachment
double-bladed knife

Ingredients
1 small onion
2 tablespoons wine or tarragon vinegar
1 egg
1 egg yolk
4 oz (100 g) unsalted or lightly salted butter
½ teaspoon golden French mustard

Method
Chop the onion very finely, scrape out and add to the vinegar in a small saucepan. Bring to the boil and cook until the vinegar is reduced by half. Combine the egg, egg yolk and the mustard in the bowl, and process for 3 seconds. Melt the butter in a separate saucepan and with the motor running pour it, foaming, but not brown, into the egg mixture. Process for 3 or 4 seconds until smooth and then add to the onion and vinegar reduction. Stir until blended and heat through over a medium to low flame until the mixture thickens. Like *hollandaise*, its fairly close relative, this sauce shouldn't be kept waiting much more than 10 minutes.

Hollandaise

Despite its Dutch name this is another French sauce. It is particularly delicious with fish and light dishes, especially chicken ones. It's a sauce which traditionally takes 20 minutes and total concentration. However, with a processor it only takes 2 minutes from scratch.

Attachment
double-bladed knife

Ingredients
1 egg
1 egg yolk
4 oz (100 g) unsalted or lightly salted butter
teaspoon lemon juice
salt and pepper

Method
Cut the butter into chunks and melt it in a small saucepan until it foams, but don't let it turn brown. Put the egg, the egg yolk, the lemon juice, a pinch of salt and pepper into the bowl and process them for 5 seconds. Then with the machine on pour in the foaming butter through the feed tube, process it for 3 seconds until smooth, tip the mixture back into the saucepan and without putting it back on the heat, stir gently allowing the heat from the saucepan to thicken the sauce. Don't leave it too long otherwise you might get scrambled eggs. You can keep the sauce warm once it is thickened in a bowl placed in hot or almost boiling water. Don't let it boil as once again the sauce might curdle. It should be eaten as quickly and as fresh as possible; it is lovely on smoked salmon, terrific on new potatoes but for asparagus or artichokes there is just nothing like it.

Sauce Maltaise

A variation is to add a tablespoon of blood-orange juice instead of the lemon juice when making it. This produces a pink coloured *hollandaise* with an orange flavour and is known as *sauce maltaise*, after the island where the oranges are supposed to have originated. It's particularly nice with asparagus.

PEANUT SAUCE

This sauce is known all over the world as saté sauce. It originated somewhere in the Indonesian Islands many hundreds of years ago, and spread to Thailand and Malaysia in the first instance, and then to Australia. It is very easy to make. I am going to give two versions, one the authentic and one the quick crafty version and it is wonderful on all kinds of kebabs, barbecues, grills or just eaten on its own with a spoon rather like a kind of sumptuous peanut butter.

SATÉ SAUCE

Attachment
double-bladed knife

Ingredients
6 oz (175 g) peanuts
1 tablespoon oil
2 tablespoons each lemon juice, brown sugar and soy sauce
1/4 teaspoon chilli powder
1 oz (25 g) coconut cream (this is sold in packets in supermarkets or health food stores, about the same size and consistency as a bar of soap)

Method
Fry the peanuts in the oil gently until they smell roasted or cooked, allow to cool and rub off the skins if there are any. Place them in the bowl and process in three bursts of 5 seconds until they are finely chopped, remove from the bowl add to a saucepan with the remaining ingredients and one cup of water, stir and bring gently to the boil. The sauce will not look very prepossessing at this stage but should suddenly turn glossy and thick. At this point you may want to adjust it for thickness. It should be about the consistency of double cream; if it is too thin, boil it for a little longer; if it is too thick, thin it with a little more water and allow the sauce to reform its glossiness. You can store it in the fridge for up to 24 hours and should serve it hot on steaks and grills but particularly on chicken kebabs.

CRAFTY SATÉ SAUCE

Attachment
double-bladed knife

Ingredients
4 tablespoons crunchy peanut butter
1 dessertspoon soft brown sugar
1 tablespoon lemon juice
1 tablespoon soy sauce
1/2 teaspoon chilli sauce
1 cup water

Method
Put the ingredients into a saucepan all together and bring gently to the boil until the peanut butter begins to melt. Transfer to the processor and blend until smooth, return to the saucepan and cook until the sauce becomes glossy and smooth. Serve warm as above.

PLUM SAUCE

This is a Chinese-style sauce used when eating Peking duck originally, but I think equally delicious on all kinds of crisp roast poultry when you are looking for something a little different from stuffing and gravy. It is really a kind of hot chutney. In a classic form it is spread on little pancakes, filled with crispy roast duck and rolled up to be eaten by gourmet diners. The sauce uses plums. If it is the wrong season or if you haven't got any to hand you can use tinned plums – but make sure they are tinned in their own juice, not in syrup.

Attachment
double-bladed knife

Ingredients
1/2 lb (225 g) cooked red plums (if fresh simmer for 20 minutes with half their weight of sugar)
2 cloves garlic
1 tablespoon oil
1/2 teaspoon chilli powder
2 tablespoons soy sauce

Method
Drain the plums from the liquid they were cooked or tinned in and make sure you have removed all the stones. Place them in the blender with the other ingredients and process until smooth; return to a saucepan and cook until the sauce has a gloss on its surface. It can then be bottled in clean sterilised bottles and kept, preferably in the fridge, for up to a month. Use it with roast duck or any other poultry or meat that has a really crisp surface.

TOMATO COULIS

This is really a sauce which Italy claims by right. At its worst it can be a nasty oily preparation, but at its best it's one of the most versatile of all sauces, to be eaten on its own with some freshly cooked pasta and grated Parmesan.

Attachment
double-bladed knife

Ingredients
1 medium sized onion
4 tablespoons olive oil (sunflower oil will do)
1 lb (450 g) Italian tinned tomatoes
1 teaspoon basil
1/2 teaspoon oregano
1/2 teaspoon sugar
salt and pepper

Method

Peel and cut the onion into quarters. Process until finely chopped. Scrape out into a saucepan in which you've heated the oil, and fry gently until soft and golden. Add the tin of tomatoes, breaking the fruit open gently with a wooden spoon. Add the sugar, salt and pepper. Simmer gently for 25 minutes, with a lid on the saucepan held open by a wooden spoon. Pour the mixture into the bowl (which it wasn't necessary to wash) and process for 5 seconds. Scrape the sides of the bowl down; add the herbs and process 3 seconds more until the sauce is smooth but still has some texture left. It can be stored before use in the fridge in sealed containers or kept in the deep freeze.

TOMATO SAUCE

This sauce is more Italian in flavour and makes use of a relatively new import to this country – passata. This is sieved puréed Italian tomatoes with nothing added but a pinch of salt. It makes a wonderful basis for a crafty sauce because it allows you to add fresh tomatoes to it (our tomatoes are always so anaemic that they need the support of something sun-ripened to give them a real Mediterranean flavour) and thereby create a sauce that has an authentic, fresh taste.

Attachment
double-bladed knife

Ingredients
¾ pint (½ litre) passata
½ lb large ripe tomatoes
2 cloves garlic
2 tablespoons olive oil
a piece from each of oregano, thyme and basil
1 tablespoon fresh parsley

Method

Peel and chop the garlic and fry it in the oil adding the quartered fresh tomatoes. Cook until the tomatoes have softened, add the passata and simmer for 15 minutes. Add the dried herbs, reserving the parsley, stir and pour into the processor, process in 3 second bursts until the fresh tomatoes are chopped up but not completely puréed, add the parsley and process again for 3 seconds until chopped and mixed into the sauce. Serve hot – it is delicious on pasta or on baked chicken and makes a terrific basis for a pizza sauce with mozzarella and black olives and anchovies on top.

Salads and Crudités

In Britain I think we are often caught between the upper and the nether millstones as far as our salads are concerned. For first courses the French have a wonderful way with what they call *crudités* – raw vegetables dressed in a variety of ways that we'd look on as salads but which they serve as *hors d'oeuvres*. As far as main course salads are concerned, the Americans have the best of it, with a series of quite amazing dishes – meals on their own. Although they vary the ingredients dramatically they manage to combine a fresh-ness, a balance of flavours and really rich dress-ings, with extraordinarily attractive presentation.

In this chapter, I have therefore concentrated on these two groups which I think can teach us all something. There's a section on French crudités, and a section on American fancy salads. Do, by the way, try the one with strawberries and cucum-bers; it may sound outlandish, but until you have tried it you just don't know what the perfect accompaniment to a summer's day (or poached salmon) can be.

Salads and Crudités

Coleslaw

Twelve years ago I wrote that coleslaw was the most famous of all American salads. That is even more true these days though I am afraid the way it is represented only too often does the original less than credit. Coleslaw originally was a simple, very finely shredded cabbage salad to which people have added in the recent years more and more complex and sometimes horrifying extras. The version here, however, is rather a special one because recent medical research has suggested that the ingredients in a common coleslaw, or in this particular case a crafty coleslaw, are incredibly beneficial in health terms. Cabbage, carrots, apples and some of the ingredients in the special coleslaw dressing I am going to suggest like honey and garlic have extraordinary good effects on disease prevention; cabbage and carrots for example have been found to be very strong inhibitors of cancer, in the case of colon and stomach cancer for cabbage and lung cancer for carrots. Garlic and honey are very good at helping to prevent blood disease and at ridding the body of the kind of cholesterol that clogs the arteries. I could go on giving you chapter and verse for each of the ingredients in this delicious salad but suffice it to say that eating it is very good for you – almost as good for you as it tastes. Please don't be tempted to use salad dressing out of a bottle – it won't taste nearly as nice or have the same beneficial effect.

Attachments
slicing and shredding disc
double-bladed knife

Ingredients
1 firm white or green cabbage (approx. 1 lb/450 g)
3 carrots
1 eating apple
1 red or green pepper

Dressing
1 clove garlic
2 tablespoons honey
2 tablespoons lemon juice
3 tablespoons salad oil

Method
Trim and clean all the vegetables, peeling the carrots but not the apple, slice the cabbage into wedges that will go into the feed tube and cut the carrots in sections that will lie flat in the feed tube. Halve the peppers and remove the seeds. Using your thinnest slicing or shredding disc, shred the cabbage and the peppers, replace the disc with a medium coarse grating disc and grate the apple and carrots on top. Tip the whole mixture into a salad bowl and mix thoroughly by hand to blend evenly. Replace the discs with the double-bladed knife, having rinsed the bowl, add all the salad dressing ingredients and

process for 3 bursts of 5 seconds until the garlic is thoroughly shredded and the honey, oil and lemon juice mixed in. You may wish to add ½ teaspoon salt to balance the dressing. Pour the dressing over the salad, mix thoroughly and leave for half an hour before serving. Some liquid will appear at the bottom of the bowl from the vegetables; stir this back into the salad to provide a proper moist and delicious texture.

Bread Salad

In the Middle East they have a rather more generous view of what makes a good salad than we tend to in Europe. Bread, after all, it not the first thing that springs to mind. But this is not only a delicious recipe, it is also extremely economical. Until you've tasted the salad, though, you must not try to adjust the seasonings to Western tastes. It may seem too lemony; but when you taste it you will find the balance actually does work, and very well. Once again without a processor it's a salad that requires a great deal of work and effort.

Attachment
double-bladed knife

Ingredients
6 thick slices of white bread
bunch of spring onions
8 oz (225 g) tomatoes
good size bunch of parsley
8 radishes
the heart of a cos lettuce
4 tablespoons salad oil
6 tablespoons lemon juice
1 dessertspoon sugar
1 teaspoon salt

Method
Put the parsley into the bowl and process until finely chopped. Add the oil, lemon juice, sugar, salt, washed and trimmed radishes, quartered tomatoes, and trimmed spring onions. Process until thoroughly blended and the vegetables are chopped into fairly small flakes. Pour into a bowl and without washing the bowl or blade, put in the slices of bread, broken into rough chunks and process until fine breadcrumbs (you may have to scrape the bowl down a couple of times). Add ½ cup of water and process again for 3 seconds to mix thoroughly. Take out and mix the breadcrumbs and the vegetable dressing. Taste for seasoning. It may need a little more liquid, in which case add up to another cup of water to moisten the breadcrumbs. Line a dish with the inner leaves of a cos lettuce and fill the centre with the bread salad.

WALDORF SALAD

This is one of those meals in a salad bowl that the Americans are so good at. It's a lovely creamy mixture of chicken, celery and walnuts, in a rather special mayonnaise.

Attachments
slicing disc
double-bladed knife

Ingredients
1 lb (450 g) boned cooked chicken meat
6 sticks celery
3 oz (75 g) walnuts
3 eating apples – preferably with different coloured skins – red and green
8 fl oz (250 ml) of mayonnaise – homemade is the nicest (see page 35)

Method
Take an ounce of the walnuts, put them into the processor with the mayonnaise and process for 10 seconds, scrape the sides down and process again until the walnuts are really finely chopped, and look like little tiny specs in the mayonnaise. (If you are making mayonnaise from scratch you can start by processing the walnuts until they are finely ground, then add the egg.) Without emptying the bowl change the double-bladed knife for the slicing disc. Wash and trim the celery and pack it vertically into the feed-tube, slice it into the bowl, followed by the apples, quartered and cored but not peeled (the coloured skins are particularly attractive in the dish). Cut the chicken meat into neat $\frac{1}{4}$ inch cubes and without processing it add to the bowl. Stir thoroughly and pile into a serving dish lined with cos lettuce leaves. Decorate with the remaining 2 oz (50 g) of shelled walnuts halved. And when you serve it make sure everyone gets their share of the nuts.

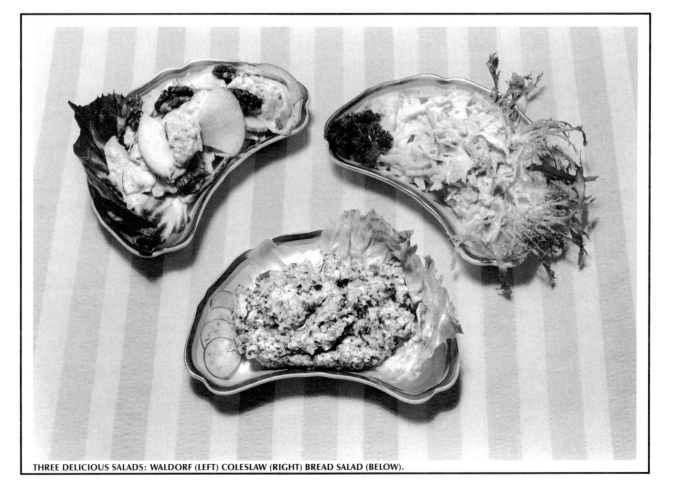

THREE DELICIOUS SALADS: WALDORF (LEFT) COLESLAW (RIGHT) BREAD SALAD (BELOW).

1&2 When slicing, hold the cucumber upright, and for the strawberries use only the weight of the plastic pusher.

3 Arrange the sliced cucumber and strawberries in overlapping concentric circles.

SALAD ELANA

One of the more exotic and exciting salads, this combines cucumber and strawberries with an orange flavoured dressing. Extraordinary though it may sound, even the black pepper sprinkled on the salad has a tradition in strawberry eating going back many years. Do try it, the combination is surprisingly delicate and delicious, and a wonderful accompaniment to almost all kinds of summer fish, and to poached, fresh salmon in particular. We can afford, or find, salmon and strawberries very rarely, but do put them together if you can, even if it's only once a year.

Attachment
slicing disc

Ingredients
½ cucumber
8 oz (225 g) large firm strawberries
8 tablespoons orange juice
2 tablespoons oil
1 teaspoon sugar
1 teaspoon salt
black pepper

Method
Score the cucumber with the prongs of a fork, all the way round in an even pattern. Top and tail it, and slice it, holding it carefully upright, through the slicing disc. Scoop out the cucumber, sprinkle it with salt and put to drain in a colander for 30 minutes. Hull and wash the strawberries, keeping aside any that are not at least an inch across for decoration later. Put the large strawberries carefully into the feed-tube and slice, using only the weight of the plastic pusher to push the strawberries through lest they become squashed. Arrange the drained and rinsed cucumber in overlapping concentric circles on a shallow dish. Lay the strawberry slices around in an equally pretty pattern, saving the smaller ones for decoration at the centre of the dish. Mix the orange juice, oil, salt and sugar (this can be done in the processor in advance, if you wish, using the double-bladed knife). Pour over the salad, making sure to coat both strawberries and cucumber thoroughly; and just before serving, grind a little fresh black pepper over the whole dish. The result is not only delicious, it is also extremely pretty.

Chinese Cabbage Salad

Although the title suggests an Eastern origin, in fact it's a salad that I've developed, using that marvellously adaptable Chinese vegetable, a cross between a cos and a savoy cabbage, that's so widely available in the shops in Britain these days and is commonly known as Chinese leaves. One of the essentials for the success of this salad is to make sure that it's really very finely sliced, which, of course, a processor makes very easy. The addition of the red pepper makes a spectacular difference to the appearance of this salad.

Do use olive oil in the dressing, – normally I don't bother, but in this case it is worth making the special effort. The tastes of the fruity oil, the crisp greenness of the salad and the rich slightly peppery flavour of the pimento, make it a very special combination indeed. Especially nice and surprising to serve at a winter dinner party when no one is expecting anything quite so fresh and attractive.

Attachments
slicing disc
double-bladed knife

Ingredients
1 Chinese cabbage
1 red pepper
3 tablespoons olive oil
$\frac{1}{2}$ teaspoon sugar
pinch salt
2 tablespoons lemon juice

Method
Cut the cabbage into quarters lengthwise, take out the heart section at the bottom, and if it's the right size place each quarter into the feed-tube and slice down. If it's still too big you may only need half of the cabbage to feed four people, then cut it into eighths and slice it vertically through the feed-tube so you get very thin ribbons. Take out and pile into a bowl – white china is very pretty with the shades of green that the cabbage produces sliced like this. Cut the pepper in half, take out the seeds, pack the halves inside each other and slice those through the disc as well. Spread the pepper slices over the top of the cabbage. Change to the double-bladed knife, put the dressing ingredients into the bowl and process to mix. Just before serving pour the dressing over the salad, don't toss it until you actually serve it, as that will disturb the prettiness of the colours and destroy one of the pleasures of this, my favourite winter salad. (If you don't eat it all at once, it will survive if kept quietly in the fridge, for about another 12 hours.)

Florida Fruit Plate

A straight steal this, from the most expensive hotel on the Miami Beach. My first real experience of the different way that Americans in general and Floridians, in particular, treat fruit and vegetables when they're turning out a salad. Do make sure that each ingredient is kept just a little bit separate and set up really decoratively around the plate. I'm going to suggest a series of ingredients but you can modify them to suit your purse and the availability in the shops.

Attachments
slicing disc
double-bladed knife

Ingredients (for 2 people)
1 avocado
bunch of radishes
1 peach
1 small punnet of strawberries
2 apples
1 pear
bunch of white grapes
3 sprigs of mint
1 carton sour cream or plain yoghurt
1 carton banana yoghurt
lemon juice
salt and pepper

Method
Halve the avocado, remove the stone, and peel it carefully. Cut each half lengthwise, into $\frac{1}{4}$ inch strips without severing the butt end of the avocado completely, and gently spread each half into a fan. Put in the centre of an oval plate and sprinkle over some lemon juice. Halve but don't peel the apples, core them and slice into the bowl. Dip them into a little lemon juice, to stop them going brown, and arrange them also in fan shapes, around the plate. Wash and trim the radishes and slice them, having packed them all into the feed-tube first. Halve and stone the peach and slice that. Keep the strawberries whole, peel and core the pear, cut it in half and slice lengthwise. Arrange all the fruit in attractive patterns, around the avocado, garnishing with the grapes, radishes and mint sprigs. Change to the double-bladed knife and process the sour cream, yoghurt and seasonings until amalgamated. Spoon a little dressing over each avocado and serve the rest in a sauce boat.

FOR PHOTOGRAPH TURN TO PAGE 41.

Crudités are not really crude, as the term suggests – it is the French word for raw vegetables. Don't be afraid to experiment – the recipes here are just suggestions, although I think you'll find that they make what we regard as very ordinary, common or garden vegetables into something that looks and tastes special. Indeed, one of the pleasures of crudités is rediscovering the real flavour of foods which have been taken for granted. Eat a combination of 3 or 4 as a first course.

BEETROOT AND YOGHURT

This most despised of salad vegetables takes on a really new flavour served and dressed this way. If you grow your own beetroot it's certainly worth boiling them for this dish, but ordinary shop-bought, ready-cooked beetroot are fine. A hint, by the way, for peeling cooked beetroot – if you find the skins difficult to get off, try doing it under water; for some reason they come off far more easily without tearing up the surface of the vegetable.

Attachment
grating disc

Ingredients
8 oz (225 g) peeled, boiled beetroot
1 tablespoon lemon juice
1 tablespoon salad oil
pinch sugar
1 small carton plain yoghurt
salt

Method
Grate the beetroot into the bowl. Stir in the lemon juice, oil and sugar, and a good seasoning of salt. Leave to stand in a bowl in the fridge for the flavours to penetrate. Serve with a large spoonful of yoghurt, stirred, at the last minute into the middle of each individual serving, or piled high in the middle of the bowl of beetroot. You'll be amazed at the texture, as well as the flavour, of this dish.

FOR PHOTOGRAPH TURN TO PAGE 48 (LEFT).

MINTED CUCUMBER

Sliced cucumber should hardly need an introduction to this country where it was immortalised in tiny brown bread and butter sandwiches with their crusts cut off; but although the French also slice it up, they treat it in rather a different manner.

Attachment
slicing disc

Ingredients
1 whole cucumber
sprig of fresh mint
1 teaspoon salt
4 tablespoons natural yoghurt

Method
Hold the cucumber carefully and, taking a fork with sharp, firm prongs, run them down the length of the cucumber. Turn the cucumber round until all sides of it are thoroughly scored. This helps the cucumber drain itself of excess liquid, and also provides an extremely pretty pattern when it's sliced across. To achieve this, place the cucumber upright in the feed-tube with the slicing disc in position. Switch on and feed the cucumber in by hand until it vanishes into the tube; finish with the plastic pusher. Switch off and you will find a whole series of very fine cucumber flowers. Mix the salt with these and put them to drain in a colander for half an hour. Bury the sprig of mint in the middle of the cucumber piled into a serving dish. Just before serving, take out the mint and stir in the yoghurt. You can serve it without having drained the cucumber, but it very rapidly becomes watery, even just sitting on the table for 5 minutes.

CARROTS WITH MEUX MUSTARD

Carrots in France are usually associated with Vichy, down towards the South West, where the spring water that they are supposed to be best cooked in comes from. There's a recipe for Carrots Vichy on page 79, but this recipe is associated with a town a bit further north called Meux where that lovely crunchy French mustard with lots of bits in it is made. For the dressing you can use bought mayonnaise, or, easiest of all, use the processed mayonnaise from page 35, adding the mustard as directed in the recipe.

Attachments
double-bladed knife
grating disc

Ingredients
1 lb (450 g) carrots
8 tablespoons mayonnaise
1½ tablespoons Meux 'whole grain' mustard
small bunch parsley

Method
Chop the parsley, scrape it out of the bowl and reserve. Fit the grating disc, peel the carrots and trim them so that they fit into the feed-tube lying on their sides lengthwise. This is in order to produce long curling slivers of carrots, rather than short, blunt ones. It doesn't make much difference to the taste, but a lot to the appearance of this dish. Grate all the carrots in the same manner. Mix the mustard and mayonnaise together, and turn the carrot slivers firmly in this until all are well coated. Transfer into a serving dish and sprinkle with the parsley. This does not need to be kept very long before it is eaten, although it will last well in the fridge for up to 6 hours.

CELERY AND WALNUT

This is a flavour combination that comes from the heart of France where walnut trees are so common they even press oil from the nuts and use it as a salad dressing. If you can find any, and are rich enough to afford it, it makes a wonderful addition to this recipe. If not, ordinary oil will do, and ordinary walnuts; the more white the celery though, the better, as the green, rather stringy variety really doesn't go terribly well in this recipe.

Attachment
slicing disc

Ingredients
1 head celery
2 oz (50 g) shelled walnuts
4 tablespoons oil
2 tablespoons lemon juice
1 teaspoon Dijon mustard

Method
Wash and clean the celery, stripping off all the leaves, but retaining those from the heart section. Pack the celery sticks tightly into the feed-tube, switch on and push the celery sticks down evenly so they all slice across the grain. Stop the motor and repeat until all the celery is used up. Break up the shelled walnut halves by hand, and crumble them over the celery in a bowl (retaining 1 or 2 for decoration). Mix the oil, mustard and lemon juice together; dress the celery and walnuts; decorate with the whole walnut halves, and allow 20 minutes for the flavours to blend.

OPPOSITE: A SELECTION OF FRENCH-STYLE CRUDITÉS: CARROTS WITH MEUX MUSTARD (TOP), BEETROOT AND YOGHURT (CENTRE) AND CELERY AND WALNUT (FRONT)

Courgette Remoulade

This is an adaptation using a modern favourite, the courgette, of a recipe that used to be made in France using celeriac, that solid swede-like vegetable with the flavour of celery. If it is winter and you can't find courgettes, revert to celeriac – you'll find it makes a very satisfactory winter crudité. My preference, however, is for the very light and delicate flavour that courgettes, which you can buy most of the year these days, give this particular dish.

Attachments
coarse grater or shredder
double-bladed knife

Ingredients
8 oz (225 g) courgettes
1 cup processor mayonnaise
2 tablespoons of parsley
1 medium sized sweet and sour gherkin
1 spring onion

Method
Top and tail the courgettes and cut them into 2 inch lengths. Fit the coarse shedder or julienne cutter on your processor. Fit the courgettes horizontally into the feeder tube and shred them. Put into a bowl, replace the disc with a chopping blade and finely chop the parsley, gherkin and spring onion. Add that to the mayonnaise and pour the sauce, which is now called remoulade, over the courgettes. Stir and serve. Don't leave this standing too long as courgettes tend to lose quite a lot of liquid and the sauce might become a little runny.

Raita

This isn't really a crudité so much as an Indian style raw vegetable salad. It's delicious eaten as a crudité and even nicer eaten as a part of an Indian meal as the mouth cooler and palate refresher, and will go with the tandoori chicken recipe you will find on page 62.

Attachment
shredding disc

Ingredients
1 green pepper
2 inch piece cucumber
2 firm ripe tomatoes
2 spring onions
1/2 lemon
6 oz (175 g) plain yoghurt
1/2 teaspoon paprika
salt

Method
Clean the vegetables and cut the green pepper in half. Feed the vegetables through the feeder tube onto your thinnest shredding disc. You can do them all into the bowl one after the other. With the spring onions, feed them in vertically so that they get sliced very thinly. Squeeze the lemon and stir it into the yoghurt with the salt. Add the sliced vegetables and stir thoroughly. Sprinkle with the paprika and leave to mellow in the fridge for at least half an hour – up to 6 hours is fine.

Exciting Eggs

Eggs have been having a lousy press recently one way and another. Many people have stopped eating them or using them as freely as they did before. I hope that the reasons for that scare are over now and that everybody has learnt a few lessons from it because eggs are absolutely fundamental to almost all forms of good cooking. Despite their importance, they are, in many ways, the least respected of foods if you think about it. Egg and chips is almost a symbol of not bothering to cook anything properly. Yet few of us would really care to eat without eggs – no more sponge cakes, or scrambled eggs, no more soufflés, no more béarnaise sauce, no more egg and chips – what a horrifying thought, especially if the chips are being produced effortlessly with a chipping disc on your processor! I don't think that such extreme measures are going to be necessary with the new caution everyone is exercising. So here are some delicious egg recipes, old and new.

One of the areas of development in food processors has been directly concerned with eggs. There was a time when food processors had a weakness with regard to eggs and that was that they couldn't beat the whites properly because most of them didn't come with the right attachments. That's no longer the case and all processors now come with a device that helps you whip egg whites to an amazing firmness. In fact the great danger is over-beating them when you are using the processor because grainy egg whites are almost as bad as under-beaten ones. If you take care, you can enjoy some of these delicious and I think egg-straordinary dishes.

Cheese Soufflé

Soufflés are often held to be extremely difficult things to make. In some ways they are because they require a little bit of precision and care, but in other ways they are really very simple to do, no more difficult, once you have mastered the knack, than making a good omelette. There are three key things: firstly, make sure the oven is at the right temperature, 400°F, 200°C, gas mark 6 is right – if you have a fan oven you may find that 190–195°C works better. Secondly, whip the egg whites so that they are exactly right, standing firmly in peaks but not grainy; and last, fold, not stir or whip the egg whites into the mixture so that they keep as much air in them as possible, this is what is going to make the soufflé rise. Do make sure that the dish you use is the right size. These recipes are for 7 inch dishes – the thin, porcelain kind with corrugated sides are best as they allow the heat to get to the food quickly. Big heavy pudding basin type dishes really aren't that suitable. Make sure that the dish is at least 3 inches deep to give the soufflé room to rise safely.

Attachments
grating disc
egg whisk

Ingredients
1 oz (25 g) plain flour
1 oz (25 g) butter
¼ pint (150 ml) milk
½ teaspoon mustard powder
4 oz (100 g) mature cheddar or 3 oz (75 g) Parmesan
4 egg yolks
3 egg whites
spare tablespoon Parmesan, finely grated
salt and pepper

Method
Preheat the oven to 400°F, 200°C, gas mark 6 (see above). Put the egg whites into the processor with the egg whisk and process until firm and in peaks but not grainy. Scoop out into a large mixing bowl and set aside. Grate the cheese into the bowl (you do not need to wipe it clean first) and set that aside. Mix the flour, milk and butter together in a non-stick saucepan with a whisk, bring gently to the boil whisking steadily. Add the mustard powder and season with salt and pepper and when thick, stir in the grated cheese. Allow to cool for 1 minute off the heat and add the egg yolks, one by one, stirring in thoroughly (you can do this in the processor with the double-bladed knife if you wish). When all the egg yolks are added, allow the mixture to cool again for another couple of minutes and then fold in the egg whites in the large bowl, trying to keep as much air as possible in the mixture. A metal spoon is best for this. Spoon into a buttered soufflé dish (see above), and sprinkle with the remaining finely grated Parmesan. Put in the middle of the preheated oven and allow to bake for 30–35 minutes until risen and golden. Bring it onto the table gently and cut it only when you and your guests are ready. The outside should be crisp and golden and the inside still creamy and moist.

Chocolate Soufflé

This is the most wonderfully rich pudding. It requires a moment or two's attention about 35 minutes before you are ready to eat it, but if you can sneak away from your guests or even your family it's certainly worth the trouble. Do use the darkest bitterest chocolate you can find – you'll find it makes all the difference to the quality, texture and taste of the soufflé.

Attachments
double-bladed knife
egg whisk

Ingredients
3½ oz (85 g) plain chocolate
2 tablespoons of orange juice
4 egg yolks
5 egg whites
2½ oz (63 g) caster sugar
1½ oz (40 g) plain flour
½ pint (300 ml) milk or semi-skimmed milk

Method
Put the chocolate, broken up, into the orange juice and put both in a small non-stick saucepan and heat over the lowest possible heat, stirring until the chocolate has melted. Put the egg whites into the processor with the beater and beat until firm but not grainy. Empty the bowl and set the egg whites aside – you do not need to wash the bowl. Put the bowl back on the machine with the double-bladed knife. Whisk together the egg yolks and caster sugar, add the flour and pour in the melted chocolate. Process for 5–7 seconds until thoroughly mixed in. Heat the milk in the saucepan which you have used for the

chocolate and pour that in and process thoroughly for 10 seconds. Pour back into the saucepan and heat over the lowest heat until the mixture thickens. Leave it to cool and fold the egg whites into the chocolate mixture very gently using a metal spoon. Pour into a 7 inch oiled soufflé dish and bake in the middle of a preheated 400°F, 200°C, gas mark 6 oven for 30–35 minutes until fully risen. People have been known to serve this soufflé with whipped cream. I wouldn't care to endorse it for health reasons but if you think you can get away with it – wow!

SOUFFLÉ OMELETTE

If a full scale soufflé seems to be a little bit more than you care to manage on a weekday night with the family to feed, try this soufflé omelette. Not quite as grand but very delicious and a marvellous vehicle for homemade jams if you happen to go in for that kind of cookery as well. You need a solid, well heated omelette pan for this and don't be tempted to make it in a large one either. 7 inch is the right size for an omelette for two people, so if you have got more to feed make more omelettes.

Attachments
egg beater
double-bladed knife

Ingredients (for 2 people)
2 eggs, separated
1 tablespoon caster sugar
1 oz (25g) unsalted or slightly salted butter
2 tablespoons strawberry or damson jam

Method
Whisk the egg whites in the processor until firm but not grainy. Set aside into a bowl. Use the double-bladed knife (you do not need to wash the bowl) to process the egg yolks and the caster sugar until lemon coloured. Fold the egg yolks and egg whites together. In a 7 inch omelette pan heat the butter until it foams and stops sizzling. Pour in the egg mixture and smooth level with a palate knife. Turn the heat down to moderate and allow to cook for 2 minutes. It will foam and swell up. Put the pan under a heated grill for just under a minute until the top sets. Spread the jam on one half of the omelette and fold over. It will look like a very fat apple turnover. Serve on warm plates immediately.

CAROLINE'S CHEESE PUDDING

I must admit that soufflés have always been a great mystery to me. It's not that I can't make them, I'm just not quite sure why anyone bothers, because they always seem to be so insubstantial that one goes chasing after them rather like clouds, never quite catching up with either their texture or taste. This dish is a primitive soufflé, taught me by an old friend called Caroline, the lady of the title. While there's nothing insubstantial about this dish, either in its texture or its flavours, the ingredients must make it one of the cheapest family favourites on record.

Attachments
grating disc
double-bladed knife

Ingredients
2 thick slices of bread (stale is OK as long as it's not rock hard)
4 oz (100 g) cheese
2 eggs
½ pint (300 ml) milk
salt and pepper

Method
Grate the cheese into the bowl; take it out and keep it. Change to the double-bladed knife. Put in the bread, broken into chunks, process until fine bread-crumbs. Take them out and mix these lightly with the cheese. Separate the eggs and add the yolks to the bowl (which doesn't need to be washed) with the milk and a generous seasoning of salt and pepper. Process for about 3 seconds until thoroughly mixed, add to the breadcrumbs and cheese mixture and then whip the whites with a beater until stiff but not grainy. Mix these carefully into the pudding and pile it all into a buttered baking dish with the sides at least an inch higher than the mixture before it's cooked. Put it into a medium oven, 375°F, 190°C, gas mark 5, for approximately 45 minutes, until a skewer or sharp knife, slid into the middle, comes out clean. It'll rise, though not so spectacularly as a true soufflé, the top will go brown and bubbly and there will be a delicious cheesy smell coming from the oven. Resist eating it until the skewer comes out clean, and then eat it quickly, with perhaps a green salad, or some fruit to follow it.

A variation that I'm particularly fond of, although Caroline hasn't authorised it, is to add a handful of chopped, *fresh* herbs (use the double-bladed knife to chop them, of course) – parsley, marjoram and chives are my favourites for this. The herbs stay green, and add a lovely fresh, country flavour to the whole pudding. Dried herbs just don't seem to work quite so well.

1 **Place the egg yolks, milk, salt and pepper into the bowl and process for 3 seconds.**

2 **Add to the breadcrumbs and cheese mixture.**

3 Whip the egg whites until stiff and mix carefully into the pudding.

4 Place in a buttered baking dish.

CAROLINE'S CHEESE PUDDING IS IDEAL SERVED WITH SALAD.

EGG MOUSSE

A very crafty starter this, made from ingredients you can keep easily in the fridge and in the store cupboard. Don't let on how easily it's made, though, because that would give the game away, and one of the pleasures of crafty cooking is that people think that far more effort is involved than actually is. That way, they get to feel cosseted and you get to put your feet up. The perfect combination!

Attachment
double-bladed knife

Ingredients
3 hard-boiled eggs
2 spring onions or small sprig of chives
1 teaspoon lemon juice
1 tin consommé (it must be one that can be served cold as a jelly)
6 tablespoons mayonnaise – homemade is best (see page 35)

Method
Melt the consommé gently but do not bring to the boil, add the lemon juice and reserve. Chop the green and white parts of the spring onions or the chives in the bowl then without taking the herbs out add the halved hard-boiled eggs and process for 5 seconds until chopped. Scrape down the sides of the bowl, add the consommé which should be cool, and the mayonnaise. Process all together for another 3–5 seconds until thoroughly mixed. Pour the whole mixture, when you have tasted it for seasoning, into a soufflé dish, and put in the fridge to chill for at least 2 hours. The consommé should set completely before you serve it. It's nicest spooned out of the dish and eaten with wholemeal or granary toast. The eggs should be left in large enough pieces to give a little bit of bite to the otherwise smooth and creamy mousse.

SMOKED SALMON SCRAMBLE

Another example of how processors make a little luxury go a long way is this trick with smoked salmon. I use it as a favourite starter for special parties; in which case serve it either on a carefully stamped out toast round (crusts removed and cut with one of those crinkly-edged cutters) or piled into the smallest, most delicate china bowls you've got. Either way, it's definitely 'ooh and ahh' time. And for a personal treat, when there's no one else around, it's not only delicious but extremely quick – and you don't have to cut the toast in fancy ways.

Attachment
double-bladed knife

Ingredients
2 oz (50 g) smoked salmon
6 eggs
1 tablespoon lemon juice
2 oz (50 g) butter
1 tablespoon processor-chopped parsley
salt and pepper

Method
Many shops that sell smoked salmon have packages of cheap off-cuts which are fine for this, as it's the flavour, not the long, thin slices, that matters.

Keep aside 2 or 3 slivers of smoked salmon, and add the rest to the bowl with the eggs and seasonings (but not the parsley). Process for 5 seconds, scrape down the sides and process again until the smoked salmon is chopped extremely finely into the egg mixture. Melt the butter in a thick saucepan, but please don't be stingy with it, the quantity is important. When it's melted, but not browned at all, add the eggs and scramble gently stirring with a wooden spoon, until they are soft and creamy but not set hard. They will go on cooking when you take them off the heat. Pile them either onto the buttered toast rounds or into small china ramekins, or even giant egg cups. Sprinkle the parsley on the top, decorate with the reserved smoked salmon pieces and serve quickly while it's still piping hot.

1 **Place onion and meat into bowl.**

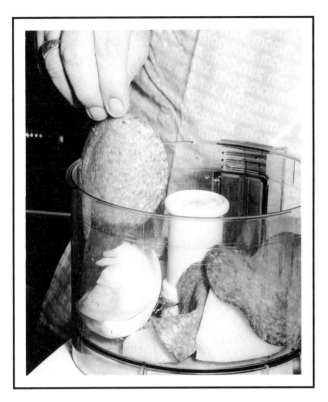

SPANISH OMELETTE

Spanish omelettes are my family's favourite and an absolutely essential part of Saturday lunchtime. This is not least because of a crafty desire to use up left-overs, and all the bits and pieces that get stuck in the fridge during the week and are still in a fit state to be consumed often find their way into this particular dish. It is possible, however, to use special ingredients which turn it into an especially tasty and visually attractive dish, but if next Saturday lunchtime you happen to have a few bits and pieces, don't be afraid to try. It's best served straight from the frying pan it's cooked in (placed on a mat on the table) in large wedges rather like a cake, and I find that with crusty wholemeal bread, lots of butter and followed by cheese and fruit it makes a good enough meal for the most hungry of families.

Attachments
double-bladed knife
slicing disc

2 **Process until coarsely chopped. Replace the knife with the slicing disc. Slice the potatoes into the mixture.**

3 **Place the eggs and seasoning into the bowl and process for 3 to 4 seconds.**

Ingredients
8 oz (225 g) cooked potatoes
1 onion
4 oz (100 g) mixed, frozen vegetables
2 oz (50 g) salami or similar cooked, cold meat
1 tomato
8 eggs
2 tablespoons oil
1 oz (25 g) butter
salt and pepper

Method
Put the peeled, quartered onion and the salami or cold meat into the bowl and process until coarsely chopped. Replace the knife with the slicing disc and slice into the mixture the cold boiled potatoes. Take a large 10 to 12 inch frying pan, put in the oil and fry the potato mixture gently until the onions are softened and the whole has a few flecks of crisp brown. Turn it over regularly. After 3 or 4 minutes add the frozen vegetables (they can still be frozen) and cook them with the mixture for another 3 minutes. Put the eggs and seasoning into the bowl and process for 3 to 4 seconds. Turn the pan heat up to hot, add a small nob of butter, and pour in the eggs, scrambling and mixing the whole panful together until the eggs start to set. Turn the heat down and leave until it's cooked through (about 4 minutes). Before serving slice the tomato thinly and place it in ring patterns on the egg.

A tasty variation, and one that stretches 8 oz (225 g) of sausages to feed 4 people, is to start by frying the sausages carefully until they are cooked through and brown, but not burst and burnt. Proceed as above leaving out the salami and when the omelette's almost set, put in the sausages cut in half lengthwise, like spokes in a wheel, and arrange the tomato slices between them. A favourite with the children this one; and pretty good for their parties too.

SERVE THIS ATTRACTIVE OMELETTE FROM THE FRYING PAN IN WHICH IT WAS COOKED.

Special Occasions

One of the great pleasures of cooking for me, is entertaining. Sometimes it's done very formally with people all dressed up and looking their best sitting round a table laden with our best crockery and cutlery. Sometimes it's friends who have just popped in to have supper round the kitchen table. Either way it's the pleasure of being with people as much as the food that makes the evening. If there is a pleasure in the food it's in sharing flavours, textures and delight in new discoveries. Here is a selection of some of my favourite special occasion food, some of it very grand and some of it for those round-the-kitchen-table dinners. It ranges from quick-fry Italian-style lamb chops, to rich and deliciously marinated Indian dishes from Kashmir. There is a dish from my native Welsh valley, honey roast lamb and

there's a really special way to serve salmon for a grand buffet party. The one important thing about all these dishes is that they are essentially main courses. Because when you are entertaining, I think it is crucial to leave enough time for the people who come to see you. That means only leaving yourself one dish to actually cook on the night and having everything else prepared as much as possible in advance. Contrasts are very important too. If the main dish is spicy, mild starters and puddings are the order of the day. If it's a creamy dish, then a crisp salad and fruit based pudding seem ideal. I hope you'll enjoy these dishes as much as I and my friends and relations have over the years. They are all main courses designed for 4 people unless the recipe specifically says 6 or more.

CHICKEN MARYLAND

Before the Colonel from Kentucky made his reputation with chicken, this style of cooking was known as 'Maryland', which is where it originally developed, in the great farm and plantation houses of that early, rich colony. At its best it is one of the most delicious ways of eating chicken; at its worst it can be a soggy, grotty mess. The secret lies in having a properly flavoured blend of homemade breadcrumbs and sufficiently hot and deep oil to get the frying right. Don't be tempted to serve the chicken with every kind of bit and piece in sight, but stick to the traditional garnish of corn fritters and flour-dipped fried bananas.

Attachment
double-bladed knife

Ingredients
1 chicken cut up into portions – or 8 chicken drumsticks, large size
3 slices of bread
1 teaspoon each tarragon and thyme
1 egg
4 tablespoons milk
1 tablespoon mustard, American for choice, English is OK but reduce the quantity to half
oil for frying

Method
If you are using a whole chicken, bone it as much as possible, or otherwise tidy up the drumsticks. Put the bread, torn into pieces, and the herbs into the bowl and process for 10 seconds, scrape down and process again for 10 seconds until you have fine breadcrumbs. Process the egg and the mustard together until smooth, then pour into a bowl. Coat the chicken drumsticks first with the egg and then with the breadcrumb and herb mixture. If there's enough breadcrumbs and egg give them a double coating. In a flat-bottomed frying pan that has a lid, heat $\frac{1}{4}$ to $\frac{1}{3}$ inch of oil until a cube of bread will brown in it in 30 seconds. Add all the chicken pieces as close together as you can – be careful of the spitting fat as you lower them in. When they have cooked for 3 minutes on each side, turn the heat down, cover with the lid and leave for another 10–15 minutes. This won't stop the outside from going crisp but it will cook the inside to a juicy perfection.

Take the chicken out, and before serving drain on kitchen paper.

SWEETCORN FRITTERS

Ingredients
4 oz (100 g) flour
1 egg
$\frac{1}{4}$ pint (150 ml) milk
1 × 11$\frac{1}{2}$ oz (337 g) can sweetcorn
$\frac{1}{4}$ teaspoon salt
black pepper
oil for frying

Method
Put the flour, salt and egg into the bowl. Turn on and, with the motor running, add the milk through the feed-tube. Process for a further 5 seconds before stopping the motor and adding the drained sweetcorn and a good grinding of black pepper. Process briefly (2–3 seconds) to mix.

Heat a couple of spoonfuls of oil in a frying pan and drop in a few spoonfuls of the fritter mixture. After 2 or 3 minutes turn the fritters to cook on the other side. Drain them on kitchen paper and keep warm while you cook the remaining fritters.

When you have finished you can add some butter to the remaining oil and fry some flour-coated bananas.

CUTLETS MILANESE

With the price of veal gone through the roof, a nice alternative to the classic Italian crispy fried fillets of veal called *Milanese*, is to do a similar thing with tender lamb chops. The combination of juicy lamb and crisp coating is delicious. Eat it either with fresh vegetables or with plainly boiled new potatoes and a garlic flavoured mayonnaise, made in the processor of course.

Attachments
double-bladed knife
grating disc

Ingredients
8 lamb chops, chined (the top bone removed and any excessive fat removed)
1 egg
2 slices of bread
4 oz (100 g) hard, dry cheese (Parmesan is best, Cheddar is OK)
1 teaspoon oregano
oil for frying

Method
Grate the cheese into the bowl. Replace the grating disc with the double-bladed knife and add the bread, torn into pieces and the oregano, and process until very fine breadcrumbs. Beat the egg, then dip each chop first into the egg, then into the breadcrumbs, repeating the process twice if you have enough egg and breadcrumbs left. The crafty way to do this is to use one hand to the wet side, i.e. the egg dipping and one hand for the dry side with the breadcrumbs. When the chops are completely coated, leave to set, preferably in the fridge, and for at least 10 minutes. Heat ¼ inch of oil in a deep, flat-bottomed frying pan until it's hot but not smoking. When you are ready to eat add the chops to the hot oil, fry quickly for 2 to 4 minutes on each side and drain on kitchen paper before serving them as suggested above.

SHRIMPS THERMIDOR

Originally this dish was made with lobster, and if you suddenly inherit a fortune, or win the pools, you could still use lobster, but large frozen shrimps make a realistic and scrumptious substitute. The dish is called *Thermidor* after the name the French revolutionaries gave the month of August in their calendar. Thermidor was supposed to be a hot month and the sauce for this dish likewise; hot with mustard, not chilli. Served with rice this makes a very special dinner party meal indeed. You can also serve it in much smaller quantities, as a rather grand first course.

Attachment
double-bladed knife

Ingredients
1 lb (450 g) frozen shelled shrimps (the larger each individual fish the better)
¼ pint (150 ml) milk
¼ pint (150 ml) apple juice
1 oz (25 g) flour
1½ oz (40 g) butter
4 tablespoons double cream
1 level dessertspoon mustard powder
½ teaspoon sugar
salt and pepper

Method
Put all the ingredients except the flour, shrimps and cream, into a small saucepan. Heat until warm but not boiling. Pour into the bowl, switch on and add the flour in a smooth stream through the feed-tube. Process for 5 seconds until smooth. Pour back into the saucepan and stir over a gentle heat until the sauce thickens, which it will do quite suddenly. Add the cream, turn the heat down, and simmer for 3 or 4 minutes. When you're ready to serve, add the shrimps, stir until thoroughly coated and heat for not more than 2 minutes, otherwise the shrimps tend to go rubbery. Serve it poured onto a bed of rice in a baking dish, sprinkled with just a little grated Parmesan, Gruyère or Cheddar cheese. Brown briskly under the grill for not more than 1 minute.

Welsh Honey Roast Lamb

Honey and lamb: not really such a strange combination when you think about the way we already regard redcurrant jelly or apple sauce as natural accompaniments to meat. In Wales as in China, oddly enough, they have long used a thin coating of runny honey on meat to provide a crisp caramelised surface. This is really a very easy dish for the cook because it's all done, meat and vegetables, in the one pan – another example of the knowledge our ancestors had about cooking which we unfortunately seem to have lost. What our forebears didn't have was the processor, and I think you'll find that in this recipe, as in so many others, it will make a lot of difference, saving you time and trouble whilst adding to the flavour of the final dish.

Attachment
slicing disc

Ingredients
1 shoulder lamb
4 tablespoons runny honey
1 lb (450 g) potatoes
8 oz (225 g) onions
1 lb (450 g) carrots

Method
Peel or scrub the potatoes, depending on how old they are. Peel the carrots and the onions, and cut them so that they will just fit into the feed-tube. Put in the slicing disc, feed through all three vegetables until you have a mixture of onion, carrot and potato in the mixing bowl. Take this out and place it in the bottom of a baking dish large enough to hold the whole of the shoulder of lamb. If you are fond of garlic you can at this stage insert a couple of slivers into the skin of the lamb. Place the lamb on top of the vegetables, put the dish in a pre-heated oven on the rack over the baking tray at 375°F, 190°C, gas mark 5, and roast it for 30 minutes. Slide the lamb out of the oven and spread the runny honey on it. Put it back immediately and allow to cook for another 17–20 minutes per lb, depending on whether you like your lamb rare or not. The juices from the meat and the honey drip down onto the vegetables and make the most delicious savoury bake to go with the crisply cooked and juicy lamb. It's a country dish this, but very much one for special and joyful occasions.

Tandoori Chicken

Already a firm favourite with the more sophisticated take-aways, Tandoori chicken is a dish that comes from the North of India on the Kashmiri/Punjab border. It was supposed to have reached its perfection at the courts of the Mogul emperors in Delhi. It's possible, especially with a processor and a modern oven, to make a very passable copy.

Attachments
slicing disc
double-bladed knife

Ingredients
a whole chicken, skinned and cut up into portion sized pieces
16 fl oz (440 ml) plain yoghurt
1 tablespoon Tandoori spice or curry powder
2 cloves garlic
1 large onion
if possible, a small handful of fresh mint

Method
Peel and quarter the onion, and slice it into the bowl. Remove the onion and replace the slicing disc with the double-bladed knife. Add the peeled and quartered garlic, the mint (if used), the yoghurt and the spices – use *either* the Tandoori mix *or* the curry powder, not both. Process for 10 seconds, scrape down the sides of the bowl and process again for another 3 seconds. Place the skinned chicken in a glass or china mixing bowl. Pour the onion, yoghurt and spice mixture over the top, turn it until thoroughly coated and leave in the fridge for a minimum of 2 hours; up to 12 hours is possible for a really deeply flavoured chicken. Take out of the bowl, shake the excess yoghurt mixture off and discard it. Place the pieces of chicken on a rack over a baking tray in a hot oven, 400°F, 200°C, gas mark 6, and bake for 30 minutes or until crisp and brown on the outside and cooked through. Serve with Indian bread (or Greek pitta bread), fresh yoghurt mixed with a little cucumber, mango chutney and a salad made of onion rings and tomato chunks. Encourage your guests to eat it with their fingers, it's quite the nicest way to get the best of the flavour.

OPPOSITE: ADD FINGER BOWLS TO ENCOURAGE GUESTS TO EAT TANDOORI CHICKEN WITH THEIR FINGERS.

Special Occasions

SUPRÊME OF BRAISED BEEF

In Britain, the cut we know as topside is very often used as a roast. The French, however, have another way of dealing with it which makes this rather dry piece of meat so succulent that I don't think you'll ever simply roast it again. You'll need an oval-shaped casserole for the job, either metal or earthenware, but it must not be too large and the meat should fit in without too much room to rattle around. It's the kind of meal to serve for a really special Sunday lunch, and despite the special flavours it's really so easy to prepare that it could become a regular event in your house. One of the potato dishes from central France like *pommes dauphinoise* on page 84 goes marvellously with this.

Attachment
double-bladed knife

Ingredients
3–3½ lb (1.5 kg) piece topside
4 oz (100 g) mushrooms
½ lb (225 g) onions
½ lb (225 g) carrots
3 stalks celery
⅓ pint (200 ml) apple juice
bay leaf
1 teaspoon instant coffee (don't panic, just stay with the recipe)
½ cupful processor chopped fresh parsley
2 oz (50 g) butter
salt and pepper

Method
Peel the carrots and onions and cut them and the celery into chunks. Wash the mushrooms in hot water. Put all the vegetables into the bowl and process for 10 seconds. Scrape the sides down and process again for 2 or 3 seconds until you have an even diced effect. Melt the butter in a small saucepan and fry the vegetables gently for 10 minutes. If you like it, you can add a clove or two of garlic cut in quarters at this stage. Don't let it burn. This process is called making a *duxelles*. Leave it to cool a little. Brown the beef either in a large frying pan or in the casserole, if it is cast iron. You don't need fat for this, just get the pan or the casserole really hot. Layer the *duxelles* into the base of the casserole, season and put the piece of meat on top, and pour over it the apple juice, mixed with the instant coffee – you'll have to trust me, it won't taste like instant coffee when it's finished. Season, add the bay leaf, seal tightly and cook for 1½ to 2 hours in a medium, 325°F, 160°C, gas mark 3 oven. A little bit more time won't hurt but turn the oven down once the meat's properly cooked. It should be tender, but still carvable and not totally falling to pieces. You can cook baked potatoes or the *gratin dauphinoise* in the oven at the same time. To serve it, take the meat out and put it on a warm serving dish or carving board. Stir the parsley, the remains of the *duxelles* and the juices in the pan together, adding a little extra apple juice, water, or if you're feeling very rich, cream. Bring the whole lot to the boil in a small saucepan, use a little to pour over the meat and use the rest as a delicious flavoursome gravy.

Halibut Gremolata

Gremolata is the finely chopped onion, garlic and parsley dressing that's normally put on *Osso buco*, the famous Milanese shin of veal dish. It's a sharp vigorous flavouring but I think wasted on just that one classic casserole and I tried it on a number of other dishes. The one that is perhaps the most successful is, surprisingly, this fish dish made with halibut, a meaty solid fish with a good strong flavour in its own right with a good strong sauce. Serve the halibut in pre-prepared portions with a good hefty teaspoon of the gremolata on top. Fairly simply cooked potatoes and a vegetable or salad afterwards is the best way of presenting this.

Attachment
double-bladed knife

Ingredients
4 4–6 oz (100–175 g) halibut steaks cut across the grain
1 tablespoon butter
1 tablespoon oil
8 fl oz (250 ml) fresh orange juice
1 tablespoon Worcester sauce
salt and pepper

For the Gremolata
The pared rind of one lemon
1 large or two small cloves of garlic
2 oz (50 g) parsley

Method
Heat the oil in a solid frying pan in which all the fish will go at once. Put the fish in, let it frizzle, turn the heat down and fry for 4–5 minutes depending on thickness. Turn over and cook again until the fish begins to flake easily. Add the Worcester sauce, pour over the orange juice and add the butter. Shake the pan gently until the sauce boils and blends. Lift the fish pieces out onto warm plates and pour the sauce around them. In the processor put the pared lemon peel with as much of the white pith removed as possible, the halved garlic and the parsley. Blend until very finely chopped and add a teaspoon of the mixture on top of each halibut steak. Serve hot and immediately.

Moules Marinières

Mussels cooked like this are one of the great dishes of France. There is a tiny restaurant on the quay at Boulogne which serves tiny mussels not much bigger than your thumb nail. You get a huge plateful and it takes hours to eat but the flavour is just exquisite. Although you can't buy tiny mussels like that in Britain you can now buy pre-cleaned ones which are a great boon. When you get them home put them into a big bowl of salted water, swill them around and discard any that haven't closed tight or that are broken. Check that the rest are thoroughly cleaned and cook them in the recipe below. About a pint of mussels per person is reasonable. If you are having one of those mussel feasts at the kitchen table that seem to occur at my house with some regularity, about a quart each is right. Don't forget to have a big bowl on the table to get rid of the empty shells. It is not, I think, a delicate dinner party dish but a great favourite with everyone who has tried it in more robust circumstances.

Attachment
double-bladed chopping knife

Ingredients
2 quarts mussels, cleaned and checked as above
1 medium onion
2 peeled cloves garlic
4 oz (100 g) parsley
6 fl oz (one breakfast cup) fresh apple juice
1 carton single cream (5 oz/125 g)
1 dessertspoon cornflour

Method
Peel the onion and cut it into quarters. Put these and the peeled trimmed cloves of garlic into the processor and chop until very fine. Get a large saucepan which will take all the mussels and has a close fitting lid. Put in the onion and garlic mixture and the apple juice and bring to a rolling boil. Pour in all the mussels, put on the lid, give the whole process a good shake and leave to steam over a medium to high heat for 5 minutes. Shake again, discard any mussels that haven't opened and take out the fish and put into a serving bowl. Into the juices, pour the cream and whisk in the cornflour (this can all be done in the processor if you like). Stir with a whisk until the sauce has thickened, check the seasoning and pour over the mussels. In the processor chop the parsley finely and sprinkle that over before finally serving with lots and lots of French bread.

Steak Pizzaiolla

A favourite from the part of Italy east of the Appenines (the other side from Rome), where they like their food pretty spicy and in a significantly different tradition from *spaghetti bolognese* and *pizza*. This is an unusual and piquant sauce, served here with steak, but one which goes equally well with lamb.

Attachments
double-bladed knife
slicing disc

Ingredients
4 entrecôte steaks
1 large onion
2 cloves garlic
a green, and if possible a red pepper
7 oz (175 g) tin Italian tomatoes
$\frac{1}{2}$ teaspoon sugar
1 teaspoon lemon juice
generous pinch chilli powder
1 teaspoon oregano
oil for frying

Method
Put the peeled, quartered onion, peeled garlic cloves, contents of the tin of tomatoes, herbs, spices and· seasonings into the bowl and process for 5 seconds, scrape down the bowl and process again for another 10 seconds until finely blended. Take out and reserve. Fit the slicing disc, cut the green and red peppers in half, remove the seeds, nest them together like Chinese boxes and feed through the slicing disc. In a large frying pan heat a couple of tablespoons of oil. Add the green and red pepper slices and sauté for 3 or 4 minutes. When they are soft but not cooked through, move to one side of the pan, turn the heat up and add the steaks. Sear on both sides, turn the heat down, add the tomato/onion purée, stir thoroughly and cook to the desired degree – about 5 minutes for rare, 6 for medium, $7\frac{1}{2}$–8 for well-done. Transfer the steaks to a serving dish, turn the heat up to maximum; stir the sauce thoroughly and pour it over the steaks before serving. Don't leave out the chilli powder, it's quite important to the balance of the sauce, and very, very authentic.

Saté

Eating pieces of meat grilled on skewers is a habit that exists across the world. Called *brochettes* in France, *kebabs* in the Middle East and *saté* in the Far East, they have the same basic principle, but the Eastern pieces of meat tend to be smaller and the sauces more exciting. It can often be very hard work, grinding up the ingredients in a pestle and mortar, although with a processor the days of almost instant saté sauces are upon us. And it's a flavour you shouldn't miss, equally good cooked on a barbecue or under the grill. The important thing is to keep the pieces of meat quite small and to serve each guest lots of little skewers rather than one or two great big thumping ones. I've given you two saté sauces on page 39. What I've got here are three different basic ingredients, prawn, lamb and chicken, each in its own marinade. The way to ring the changes is to stir the marinade into the saté sauce and cook it for 5 minutes before serving with the appropriate ingredient.

Prawn Saté

This is a grand and rather expensive dish but the flavours are so exquisite, it's occasionally worth the trouble and expense.

Attachment
double-bladed knife

Ingredients
$1\frac{1}{2}$ lb (675 g) raw large ($1\frac{1}{2}$–2 inch) prawns, headed
4 oz (100 g) coconut cream (bought in the block)
rind and juice of lemon
$\frac{1}{2}$ teaspoon chilli powder
1 inch piece fresh ginger
2 gloves garlic
4 tablespoons light soy sauce
1 cup (6 fl oz) water

Method
Put all the ingredients except the prawns, water and coconut cream into the processor with a double-bladed knife. Heat the water with the cream in it until melted and smooth. Pour into the marinade mixture and process again for 10 seconds until smooth. Pour over the prawns or shrimps which you can have shelled if you choose. Leave to marinate for at least 6 hours. Thread, 6 at a time, onto skewers and grill for 5 minutes a side until the flesh is white and the shells are crisped. Pour the marinade mixture into one of the saté sauce recipes and simmer for 10 minutes. Serve the prawns with the sauce under them so that people can shell the prawns before dipping them into the sauce. Finger bowls and nice big napkins are a good idea.

Lamb Saté

Attachment
double-bladed knife

Ingredients
1½ lb (675 g) of boneless fillet of leg of lamb
1 medium sized onion
1 clove garlic
1 tablespoon soft brown sugar
1 teaspoon coriander powder
1 teaspoon ginger powder
juice of a lemon

Method
Put the peeled and quartered onion and peeled and trimmed garlic in the processor with the double-bladed knife, add all the other marinade ingredients and purée to a fine paste. Cut the meat into small slices, about the size of a commemorative postage stamp and about ¼ inch thick. Put into a large bowl and add the marinade ingredients, tossing and turning to make sure they are thoroughly covered. Marinade for at least an hour, up to 12 hours is fine. Thread onto thin bamboo-type skewers and grill for 4–5 minutes a side. Add the marinade mixture to one of the saté sauces and simmer for 5 minutes before serving. Pour over the lamb skewers.

Chicken Saté

Attachment
double-bladed knife

Ingredients
4 boneless breasts or boned thighs approximately
1½ lb (675 g) in weight
2 cloves garlic
juice and grated rind of lemon
½ teaspoon each turmeric, ginger and salt
2 tablespoons light soy sauce
4 tablespoons water

Method
Put all the sauce ingredients except the chicken into the processor with the double-bladed knife and process until a smooth purée. Cut the chicken into pieces 1 inch long and ½ inch wide, about ¼ inch thick, and coat with the marinade mixture. Leave for a minimum of 1 and up to 12 hours. Thread the chicken on to bamboo-type skewers lengthwise and grill 5 minutes a side under a preheated grill or on a barbecue. Mix the remaining marinade into one of the saté sauces on page 39, simmer for 5 minutes and serve over the chicken skewers.

VENETIAN LIVER

This is the way they like to serve liver in Venice. Traditionally it uses calves' liver but as that is very expensive and difficult to find I suggest you try using lambs' liver instead. Do, however, make sure you get fresh, top quality liver, preferably in a piece so that you can slice it yourself. In this particular recipe, the liver has to be very thinly sliced and that's best done by hand. It is traditionally served with a rice and pea mixture known as *risi bisi*. You can copy it very easily by cooking rice in the normal way and adding a cupful of fresh or frozen peas to give them time to cook with the rice.

Attachment
thin slicing disc

Ingredients
1½ lb (675 g) lambs liver (hand sliced thinly into sheets)
1½ lb (675 g) large onions
3 tablespoons olive oil
3 tablespoons white wine vinegar
salt and pepper

Method
Cut the onions into halves and, using the processor, slice them as thinly as possible. In a large frying pan heat the oil and add the thinly sliced onions. At first they will seem like a very large mass but they will cook down and caramelise. Don't let them turn dark brown, they should remain a pale golden colour. The whole process should take about 15 minutes. When the onions are cooked, season them generously and put them into a warm serving dish. Pour the vinegar into the frying pan and bring to the boil. Add the thinly sliced liver and cook for just 30 seconds on each side. Put on to the onions. Pour the sauce over the whole and serve hot immediately. Don't be tempted to cook the liver longer, sliced very thin it will be tender like this, but shoe leather if cooked for twice the length of time.

CHICKEN WITH LIME, GINGER AND HONEY SAUCE

This dish makes use of the wonderful exotic vegetables available these days.

Attachments
double-bladed knife

Ingredients
4 chicken breasts
1–1½ inch piece of fresh ginger
2 cloves garlic
1 fresh lime
4 tablespoons runny honey
salt and pepper

Method
Peel the ginger and cut it into ¼ inch slices. Put these and the peeled trimmed garlic cloves into the food processor. Add a couple of tablespoons of water to help the blades work and process in 2 second bursts until finely chopped. Cut the lime in half, take out any pips, trim the ends off, cut it into quarters and add these to the processor. Process again for about 10 seconds until the lime is chopped up. Add the honey, season, and process one more time to mix the marinade together. Pour over the chicken breasts, coating them completely and leave them covered for up to 48 hours in the fridge. Heat your grill to its maximum for at least 10 minutes, put the chicken breasts on a rack and grill for 6–8 minutes on both sides until cooked right through. Heat the marinade in a separate pan until it boils and use this to baste the breasts. A little can be poured over when the breasts have finished cooking, to add a final gloss and an intense flavour to the chicken.

STEAK WITH STILTON AND MANGO CHUTNEY

I first tasted this particular recipe some years ago in a French-style steak bar behind Victoria Station in London. It was a queer place that only served steak and produced a variety of different sauces, some more or less successful to vary the menu. This particular sauce is the sort of thing that appeals to people who like their steak a little pink, because with the coating on it, it never becomes the dark ruined brown that 'well-done' always indicates.

Attachment
double-bladed knife

Ingredients
4 6–8 oz (175 g–225 g) entrecôte steaks approximately ½ inch thick
4 tablespoons mango chutney
4 oz (225 g) Stilton
½ tablespoon butter

Method
Heat the grill very hot and grill the steaks on one side for 3–4 minutes. Don't season them until after they're grilled as the salt draws the juices out of the meat. Put the Stilton, mango chutney and butter into the food processor and blend until smooth. Divide into 4 portions and spread this on the uncooked side of the steaks and replace under the grill. Cook until the filling is browned and bubbling and the steaks underneath have had a chance to heat through. This should take about 3–4 minutes. Serve immediately with potatoes and a salad as anything else would have no chance of coping with the strong and delicious flavours.

CORONATION TURKEY

This particular sauce combination was first invented, as legend has it, for the Coronation dinner of our Queen when, with so many visitors from around the world, it was difficult to produce a meal which could appeal to sophisticated palates and yet conform to the dietary rules dictated by a variety of religions and customs. In its original form the sauce was used with chicken but I think that turkey is an ideal basis for this particularly piquant sauce. It can be made up to 12 hours in advance and kept in the fridge but don't keep it longer than that both for safety's sake and also because it begins to look a little tired. It's a dish that requires piling up high on a pretty plate to make it look good in the middle of a buffet. I have lightened the sauce slightly in view of modern tastes and the availability of some of the new dairy products with a low fat base.

Attachment
double-bladed knife

Ingredients (for 8 people)
4 lb (1 kg 800 g) cooked turkey (bought ready cooked or cook one of the breast joints widely available)

For the sauce:
8 oz (225 g) mayonnaise (page 35)
8 oz (225 g) low fat fromage frais
½ pint (300 ml) milk
1 tablespoon flour
1 tablespoon butter
1 dessertspoonful curry powder
salt and pepper
4 oz (100 g) apricot jam
2 oz (50 g) slivered almonds

Method
Cook the curry powder gently for 2–3 minutes in the butter in a non-stick pan. Add the milk and the flour, stir to mix, put into the processor and blend until smooth. Return to the pan and cook until thick. Add the apricot jam to the mixture whilst it is still hot. Cool and put the whole lot back into the processor and blend until smooth adding the fromage frais and the mayonnaise in turn. Check the sauce for seasoning, it may need a little lemon juice to balance the apricot jam if it's too sweet. Cut the turkey up into 1 inch cubes and mix thoroughly with the sauce. Toss the slivered almonds in a lightly greased frying pan until they turn pale gold, sprinkle over the top and garnish when ready to serve with parsley or watercress to add a bright green contrast.

CUCUMBERED SALMON

This is an extremely pretty centrepiece for a party and always brings 'oohs and aahs'. It is very simple to make but requires some work in advance, so it is best to do the day before you plan to eat it if you can. Farmed salmon are now very plentiful, very cheap and very delicious with only a real expert being able to tell the difference between that and the wild fish. Do be sure, however, to buy one that has a bright fresh look about it with a gleaming silver skin and eyes that still have a slightly lively look.

Attachment
thin slicing disc

Ingredients (for 8 people)
1 3½ lb (1.5 kg) salmon
1 lemon
1 cucumber
2 branches watercress

Method
Put a large piece of foil big enough to take the salmon in a baking dish. Oil it lightly and, having sliced the lemon, put three slices of lemon along it and lay the salmon on top. Lay three more slices of lemon on top of the salmon (then any remaining bits can go in the cavity) and cover with another piece of oiled foil leaving a little air space around the salmon as you fold the edges together to form a parcel. Pre-heat the oven to 350°F, 180°C, gas mark 4 and bake the salmon for 12 minutes a pound, for a 3½ pound fish this would be just under 40 minutes. Switch the oven off and leave the salmon to cool in the foil without opening it, preferably overnight. When it's cool unwrap and skin the salmon gently using a sharp knife to lift the skin. You'll find it and the fins come off fairly easily. Discard the trimmings and place the fish on an oval serving dish that it fits comfortably. Put the trimmed and washed cucumber through the slicing disc of the processor, getting as thin slices as you can. Beginning at the tail end, lay these slices on to the salmon to reproduce the effect of scales with the green edge of the cucumber. Continue until you get to the head end, leaving the head itself bare. Dress the dish with the watercress and chill for up to 6 hours before serving. I think this is particularly delicious and attractive with the Salad Elana on page 44.

CHICKEN AND PEPPER STIR FRY

This is a really wonderful, quick supper when friends turn up unexpectedly. You'll need to cook the rice at the same time as you're getting this ready but as the whole lot will only take about 20 minutes from start to finish you should have dinner on the table without too much delay. If you've got the ingredients, a light bowl of clear chicken noodle or mushroom soup goes well with it. Serve it at the same time, not as a starter, so you eat and drink in the Chinese style.

Attachments
slicing disk
double-bladed knife

Ingredients
12 oz (350 g) chicken breasts or boned thighs
1 large Spanish type onion
1 red pepper, 1 green pepper
1 clove of garlic
½ teaspoon ground ginger
3 tablespoons soy sauce
1 tablespoon soft brown sugar
1 tablespoon cider or white wine vinegar
1 dessertspoon cornflour
6 fl oz (breakfast cup) water

Method
Peel the onion and cut into two halves, clean, deseed, and halve the peppers. Using the slicing disc, shred finely. Cut the chicken pieces, across the grain, into ¼ inch slices. This is best done by hand with a very sharp knife. Heat a tablespoon of oil in a large frying pan or wok if you have one. Add the crushed garlic and the ginger and then the peppers and onion mixture. Stir fry and toss for 1½ minutes, take out of the wok and put aside. Put in the chicken pieces and fry until firm and cooked. Put the vegetable mixture back in with the chicken and mix thoroughly. In the food processor with the double-bladed knife mix all the other ingredients – soy sauce, sugar, vinegar, cornflour and water – until thoroughly blended. Pour into the wok and turn the heat up high. Toss, then stir the mixture gently until the sauce thickens and goes glossy. Serve with cooked rice and a bowl of Chinese-style soup.

Marvellous Ways with Mince

Perhaps of all the tasks that the processor makes easy, mincing meat is both the most obvious and yet the most surprising. We are all used to buying 'mince' from the butcher, but this is usually made from scrag ends of beef and helps to bulk out our economy dishes and the butcher's profits. However the texture, flavour and excitement of dishes made from meat you have minced yourself gives great pleasure, and in the recipes that follow you'll find suggestions for both lamb and beef recipes. What they all share is that by chopping the meat yourself you're getting something that's of a totally different quality from the mince made by a butcher. The reason for this is simple: 'butchers' mincers' squeeze and grind the meat together to reduce it to a finely cut consistency, while a processor actually slices it. The French call it *haché*; and because it's super-sliced the quality and texture of the meat is retained. You can have coarsely ground beef for a *chilli con carné* that will be a revelation even to most Mexicans, or have lamb minced super-fine to make the most delicious of North Indian kebabs to eat with chutneys, poppadums, and all the trimmings. And for the really adventurous, a dish in which the meat is never actually cooked, the French *steak tartare*.

One note about mincing meat that applies to all these recipes: before putting it into the bowl, cut it up into even-sized pieces, and make sure there's no bone or any large chunks of gristle. The machine can cope with almost anything, but if you want smooth, evenly-minced meat you've got to start with pieces of a reasonably even size, and without anything that will stop the meat being cut into evenly-sized pieces.

STEAK TARTARE

The very description of *steak tartare*, raw minced beef with raw egg mixed into it, eaten as it stands, is not everybody's idea of a tasty meal. But it's not a coincidence that this unusual dish, named after the central Asian nomads who were supposed to have developed it, has remained a firm favourite on gourmet menus throughout the world. You have to try it before you knock it, and once you try it you'll probably love it, as I certainly do. The taste is delicate not rough, and you can almost feel it filling you with zest and vigour. One word of warning: it's remarkably filling, so don't be tempted to serve larger portions than I suggest.

Attachment
double-bladed knife

Ingredients
1 lb (450 g) rump or sirloin steak
1 onion
1 gherkin
4 teaspoons chopped parsley (done in the processor)
1 level teaspoon each, grainy French mustard, lemon juice, Worcester sauce, oil
1 whole egg
4 egg yolks
salt
freshly ground black pepper
4 drops tabasco

Method
Put the whole egg, all the seasonings and vegetables into the bowl and process for 10 seconds until smoothly puréed. Add the meat, cut into neat cubes with the fat and gristle removed, and process for another 10–15 seconds until thoroughly blended, but not chopped too fine – a little texture is important here. Remove and pat into a smooth giant hamburger shape on the serving dish. When you separate the 4 eggs, keep the yolks in a half shell, and nestle the half shells around the giant hamburger shape. You can, if you like, add some anchovy in a pattern between the eggs. Serve it as it stands for each diner to mix an egg yolk into his or her own meat. Crisp salad and a baked potato on a side plate are my favourite accompaniments. Do try it – it may even make you feel a little nomadic yourself.

HAMBURGERS

I make no apology for including this recipe for hamburgers because the texture and juiciness of the meat when minced properly makes this common dish a revelation. Don't be tempted to add any other ingredients; the basic flavour of the beef comes through far better if not too heavily disguised.

Attachment
double-bladed knife

Ingredients
1¼ lb (550 g) chuck steak
1 small or ½ large onion
1 egg yolk
1 teaspoon each, salt and freshly ground black pepper
oil for frying

Method
Cut the meat into even-sized cubes, leaving on any fat but removing all gristle. Process for 10 seconds, scrape down the sides; flash the motor on and off again to make sure it's all thoroughly evenly cut, then turn into a separate bowl. Add the onion and egg yolk to the bowl and process until puréed, add to the meat with the salt and pepper. Mix all the ingredients thoroughly together, divide into 4 and shape into 1 inch thick patties with smooth, round sides. Let these stand, if you can, in the fridge for a few minutes, and then barbecue them or fry them in a minimum of oil in a thick bottomed frying pan. If you like them rare, a minute on each side on high and then 5 minutes over a low flame will do it; if you like them a little bit better done, a minute on each side on high and 7 to 8 minutes on low is about right. You can eat them in buns, with the traditional gherkins, tomato sauce, mustard and relishes.

CAMBRIDGE STEAK

Add a little lemon juice and Worcester sauce to the juices in the pan and serve the patties as a dish in their own right with potatoes and vegetables, pouring the sauce over them. Hamburgers served like this are called a variety of names, some grand and some humble, but Cambridge Steak is the one I've heard used the most.

PARTY HAMBURGERS

Attachment
double-bladed knife

Ingredients (for 12 hamburgers)
4 thick slices of bread
2 large onions
1½ lb (675 g) chuck steak
6 fl oz (1 breakfast cup) water
6 tablespoons tomato ketchup
1 tablespoon Worcester sauce

Method
Make breadcrumbs with the bread cut into 1 inch chunks in the processor, tip out and add the meat cut into 1 inch cubes with any gristle or hard bits carefully removed. Mince the meat so that it is still coarsely minced, add the onions, peeled, quartered and cut into ½ inch slices. Process for 10 seconds until they are mixed with the meat. Add the breadcrumbs and all the other ingredients and process in 3 bursts of 5 seconds until thoroughly mixed. Season generously. Test for texture – the mixture should be firm but pliable. Chill for ½ an hour in the fridge before shaping into 12 patties for grilling, frying or oven baking at a high temperature 400°F, 200°C, gas mark 6. They can be frozen after they're made if you started with fresh meat in the first place. They shouldn't be kept for more than a month, however, at normal domestic freezer temperatures.

LAMB BURGERS

This variation uses lamb instead of beef, a useful alternative in the light of recent uncertainties. Lamb can be fatty when you buy it so make sure you trim off any obvious and excessive chunks of fat before putting the meat in for mincing. If you can find some of the older lamb, hoggit or even mutton which is sometimes available these days, it also makes wonderful burgers.

Attachment
double-bladed knife

Ingredients (for 4 hamburgers)
1 lb (450 g) of trimmed boneless lamb (shoulder or best end of neck is fine)
1 clove garlic
piece of dried rosemary
1 dessertspoon soy sauce
1 tablespoon cornflour

Method

Trim the lamb and cut into 1 inch cubes, put into the processor and process in bursts of 5 seconds until reasonably finely minced. Sprinkle the cornflour over the meat and add the garlic (cut in half), soy sauce and rosemary. Process for another 3 bursts of 3 or 4 seconds until it is all thoroughly blended. Allow to chill for half an hour in the fridge and shape into 4 oval-shaped patties. Grill or shallow fry for 4–5 minutes a side. Serve either in buns or on their own with salad and rice or potatoes.

LAMB KEBABS

This dish is from the Middle East, though variations are to be found from Morocco to Afghanistan. They can be difficult to make in the traditional way – however, a food processor makes things very simple.

These unusual minced kebabs are delicious served either as an Eastern sandwich inside Greek pitta-type bread or an Indian chappati; or as a main dish on a plate with rice or fried potatoes, which are so dear to the Turks' hearts. Don't be afraid to experiment with other flavourings and herbs if you fancy a bit more of a culinary cook's tour.

Attachments
double-bladed knife

Ingredients
1 lb (450 g) boneless lean lamb or mutton
1 tablespoon rice flour (or ground rice)
1 tablespoon lemon juice
1 teaspoon Worcester sauce
1 teaspoon curry powder
1 teaspoon garlic salt
1 peeled onion
salt and pepper

Method

Cut the lamb into cubes and put it into the bowl with all the other ingredients. Process for 20 seconds, scrape down the sides and process again until the mixture is really smooth. This is traditionally done with a pestle and mortar and takes at least an hour to get the necessary smooth consistency. When finished, shape into rolls, about 4–5 inches long and 1 inch thick and put these, if there is time, in the fridge to chill for $\frac{1}{4}$ hour. Thread each one separately onto a skewer, and grill under a preheated grill or barbecue for 5 minutes each side.

CHILLI CON CARNÉ

This is almost regarded as the national dish of Mexico, although its real origins are rather further north, and it has at least as much Texas as Mexico in its parentage. Nevertheless, it's another of those marvellously exotic and economical dishes which can be served either as a family supper or for a grander occasion. It's best served with rice to which you've added for the last 5 minutes of cooking a packet of frozen sweetcorn (thus saving on washing-up as well). In California, where Mexican food is a new-found fashion, they sometimes serve it with a separate bowl of sour cream which is unusual, but, like so many things Californian, quite nice when you try it.

It is important in this recipe not to over-mince the meat, because a certain 'bitey' texture is quite important to the finished dish.

Attachment
double-bladed knife

Ingredients
1 lb (450 g) chuck steak
2 tablespoons oil
8 oz (225 g) onions
1 teaspoon each, cinnamon, ground cumin, paprika and pinch of cayenne pepper
or 1–2 teaspoons chilli powder
1 × 16 oz (450 g) tin tomatoes
1 × 16 oz (450 g) tin red kidney beans (baked beans won't do for this one)
salt and pepper

Method

Cut the meat into 1–1½ inch cubes and process lightly for 2 or 3 seconds, until the meat is minced but still in discernible pieces (this is really a stew, not a kind of soup). Fry the mince in a big pan in a couple of tablespoons of oil until it's well browned. Put the onions into the bowl and chop finely, and add the tin of tomatoes through the feed-tube with the motor running. Stir the spices into the meat, and season with salt and pepper. You can add a teaspoon of oregano at this stage (it's very much an optional extra, even in Mexico). Add the tomato and onion mixture then bring to the boil before adding the contents of the tin of beans. Turn the heat down to low; cover and simmer gently for at least half an hour. The longer this dish cooks the better it tastes, and an hour is ideal. It will turn a dark rich red and the beans will absorb the flavour of both the meat and the herbs.

ITALIAN MEATBALLS (1)

This is one of the dishes which came about when Italian immigrants to New York earlier this century married the cooking of their homeland with the abundance of their adopted country. The result was good, country-style fare, rich in flavour and ingredients. Don't be tempted to spare the garlic – and don't expect to take violent exercise afterwards.

Attachment
double-bladed knife

Ingredients
1 lb (450 g) chuck steak
2 slices wholemeal bread
1 onion
1 teaspoon oregano
1 egg
2 cloves garlic

For the sauce
1 onion
2 cloves garlic
2 teaspoons Worcester sauce
1 teaspoon each, basil and thyme
1 large tin Italian tomatoes
3–4 tablespoons oil
2 tablespoons butter
1 teaspoon sugar
1 teaspoon lemon juice
1 lb (450 g) Italian spaghetti
salt and pepper

Method
Cut the meat into small cubes and break the bread into chunks. Peel the onion and garlic cloves. Process the meat until medium-coarse (about 7–8 seconds) then add the bread, one onion, 2 cloves of garlic, the oregano and the egg and process for 5–7 seconds or until well mixed; form into 1 inch–1½ inch meatballs and fry until lightly browned in 1 to 2 tablespoons of oil. Add the second onion and remaining garlic to the bowl, process until puréed then with the motor running add the tomatoes, the remaining herbs, the sugar, the Worcester sauce and the lemon juice and seasonings and process briefly. Melt the butter and the remaining oil in a separate saucepan; add the tomato mixture, and cook, stirring regularly for at least 10 minutes. An extra 15 minutes partially covered with a lid and on a low heat improves the flavour remarkably, as does a bay leaf if you have one. Add the meatballs to the tomato sauce, partially cover the pan, and simmer for another 15 minutes while cooking the spaghetti. When cooked arrange the spaghetti in a big ring on a large plate and pour the meatball and tomato sauce mixture into the middle.

FOR PHOTOGRAPH TURN TO PAGE 71.

ITALIAN MEATBALLS (2)

This variation on the meatball theme was originally made with veal, but both in America and in this country veal can be hard to come by and turkey breast makes a surprisingly satisfactory substitute. This dish was originally made to eat with Polenta, the Italian cornbread that comes from the Po valley region and is still popular in parts of Little Italy in New York. If you don't like or can't get Polenta, tagliatelle makes a good accompaniment.

Attachments
slicing disc
double-bladed knife

Ingredients
1½ lb (675 g) leeks
1 lb (450 g) turkey fillet or leg meat (boneless)
a slice of bread in 1 inch (2.5 cm) cubes
1 clove garlic
1 egg
8 oz (225 g) Italian tinned tomatoes
rind and juice of lemon
2 tablespoons olive oil
1 teaspoon each of basil, oregano and ½ teaspoon rosemary
salt and pepper

Method
Trim and wash the leeks extremely thoroughly to remove any sand or dirt. Fit the slicing disc to the processor and slice them thinly. Set aside and change the blades so that you now have the double-bladed knife in the processor. Cut the turkey into 1 inch cubes and put it, with the cubed bread, the peeled and trimmed clove of garlic, the rind of the lemon, the rosemary and the egg into the bowl. Process until the mixture has formed a smooth purée. Scrape down the sides and process 5 seconds more. Clean out and chill for 20 minutes in the fridge. Meanwhile fry the sliced leeks in 2 tablespoons of olive oil until they've softened. Add the tomatoes and their juice, the lemon juice, the oregano and basil, mix thoroughly and cook gently for 10 minutes. Shape the turkey mixture into 1 inch meatballs (you may find wetted hands useful for this exercise). Fry them lightly in a frying pan in a little oil until just browned and firm and add to the leek and tomato mixture. Put on a very low heat and simmer for 25–30 minutes. Check for seasoning and serve with plenty of freshly ground black pepper on 1 lb (450 g) of tagliatelle cooked as per instructions and moistened with a little butter before adding the turkey meatballs.

MEXICAN MEATLOAF

The meatloaf is a favourite American Sunday lunch, usually eaten with potatoes and vegetables, like our own Sunday roast. This variation comes from the south west of the United States where they prefer their food with rather more bite, thanks to the traditional relationship with the Mexican chilli just across the border.

Attachment
double-bladed knife

Ingredients
1½ lb (675 g) chuck steak trimmed of gristle and fat
8 oz (225 g) of red kidney beans cooked (or tinned)
1 large onion
1 clove garlic
2 eggs
1 teaspoon each cumin powder and ground cinnamon
½ teaspoon or more, to taste, chilli powder
salt and pepper

Method
Cut the meat into 1 inch cubes and process until roughly ground. Add the beans, the peeled and quartered onion, the peeled and trimmed garlic and process until mixed. 3 or 4 bursts of about 7 seconds is probably best scraping down the sides in between bursts. Add the eggs, seasoning and spices and process again. Tip into a 2 lb loaf tin and unmould on to a baking sheet and bake it at 350°F, 180°C, gas mark 4 for 45–50 minutes. Chilli sauce is a perfect accompaniment. You can buy it ready-made, or make your own by adding a little more chilli powder to the tomato salsa recipe on page 14.

Versatile Vegetables

Contrary to popular rumours the British are very good at cooking vegetables. We like vegetables, you see, and I have a vague suspicion that no one else really does. The French have an array of amazing dishes, one or two of which you will find in this chapter, but if you eat out in France you will be hard put to find them except as a gesture midst an array of fish, meat, cheese and eggs. Even in America, where salads have certainly reached very high standards, other vegetables often take a back seat. In Britain with the meat always goes two or three vegetables, and it is those recipes that are celebrated in this chapter. Most vegetable recipes are still intended to be eaten as an accompaniment to a main course, and certainly some dishes seem to have a particular affinity for each other – the *pomme Dauphinoise* for example is wonderful with roast beef, the Punchep with braised lamb, and the courgettes with grilled chicken. Some of them can also be eaten on their own as first courses or even light lunches – the sprouts Polonaise and ratatouille are two terrific examples of this. At home, I often serve 3, 4, or even 5 vegetable dishes together as a main course, with no meat or fish. A number of the dishes in this chapter could be eaten like that. I have also added a couple of Chinese-style stir-fry recipes. These are enormously popular these days, not least because like a lot of modern vegetable cookery they leave the vegetables crisp, although cooked right through. That of course doesn't apply to potatoes and there are one or two of those recipes here, too. All these dishes benefit from the use of the processor to make the preparation effortless and the results excellent. The ability to cut vegetables evenly is a key to their success and is just one of the advantages of crafty food processor cookery.

SPROUTS POLONAISE

The French have a habit of identifying styles of cooking by the countries in which they think they first met them. I don't know if anyone in Poland ever did use this lovely combination of butter-fried garlic-flavoured breadcrumbs and crumbled hard-boiled eggs, but it's a combination that I use particularly with sprouts as it brings out their nuttiness and crispness. You can serve sprouts Polonaise as a first course, with simple grilled meats, or as a supper dish in its own right with lots of wholemeal brown bread.

Attachment
double-bladed knife

Ingredients
1¹/₂ lb (675 g) sprouts
2 slices white bread
2 oz (50 g) butter
¹/₂ teaspoon garlic salt
2 hard-boiled eggs
1 tablespoon lemon juice
¹/₂ teaspoon ground black pepper
salt

Method
Clean the sprouts carefuly but do not cut the traditional cross in their base. Put them in a steamer if you have one, or if not in about 1¹/₂ inches of hot water. Add a pinch of salt, bring them to the boil and cook or steam them for not more than 7 or 8 minutes. Take one out and test it! It should be cooked all the way through, bright green and still a little crisp to the bite at the heart. Drain, then cover to keep them warm. While the sprouts are cooking, roughly break up the bread slices and process them until you have fine breadcrumbs. Melt 1¹/₂ oz (40 g) of butter in a frying pan, and stirring gently, fry the crumbs until they are golden brown. Sprinkle the garlic salt over them and set aside until the sprouts are ready. Shell the hard-boiled eggs, cut them in half and remove the yolks. Put the whites into the bowl and process until they too are finely chopped, and keep them. With a fork break up the yolks until they also resemble breadcrumbs. You can do this in the processor with a large quantity, but 2 yolks get a little lost. When all the ingredients are ready, heat up the frying pan, add another ¹/₂ oz (13 g) of butter and the lemon juice and sizzle the sprouts very quickly for about ¹/₂ minute before adding the breadcrumbs, then mix them both together. Turn into a warm serving dish and sprinkle over the egg white followed by a neat pattern of the crumbled yolk and black pepper over the top.

FOR PHOTOGRAPH TURN TO PAGE 77.

RATATOUILLE

The classic southern French vegetable dish which blends aubergines and courgettes, tomatoes, onions and green peppers, to make a superb ragoût. The virtue of the dish is that not only is it delicious at the time you cook it, but it can be eaten cold and even heats up to advantage. For me the wild thyme and lavender scented hills of Provence, with views over the deep blue Mediterranean, are conjured up every time I see and taste this evocative dish.

Attachments
slicing disc
double-bladed knife

Ingredients
8 oz (225 g) aubergines
8 oz (225 g) courgettes
8 oz (225 g) green peppers
1 red pepper
8 oz (225 g) onions
1 lb (450 g) tomatoes or 1 lb (450 g) tin Italian
tomatoes
1 clove garlic
4 tablespoons oil
1 teaspoon each, basil and oregano
salt and pepper

Method
Wash and clean all the vegetables, de-seeding the peppers carefully. Pack them into the feed-tube with the slicing disc in position and slice the onions, peppers, courgettes and aubergines (you may have to cut these in half to fit the feed-tube). Sprinkle the courgettes and aubergines with a little salt and leave them to drain for 20 minutes or so. Rinse the salt off and you're ready to proceed. Heat the oil in a deep frying pan, big enough to take all the vegetables, peel the clove of garlic, crush it roughly with a knife and put it in the oil to cook until light gold. Add all the vegetables, except the tomatoes, turn them in the oil and leave them to simmer for 5 minutes. If you're using a tin of tomatoes, simply open it and pour the contents into the processor fitted with the double-bladed knife. If you are using fresh tomatoes, just cut them in quarters before placing them in the processor. Process for about 10 seconds, until you get a coarse purée. When the vegetables in the pan have cooked for 5 minutes, season them with salt and pepper and add the tomato mixture. If it's very dry, you can add a tablespoon or two of water as it cooks, but basically the stew should cook in its own juices and in the garlic-flavoured oil. Put it over a very low heat, do not cover and leave it for about 30 minutes, turning it occasionally, then sprinkle on the herbs and test for seasoning. The vegetables should still be separate and distinguishable but have blended into a delicious soft coherent whole. The dish is nice hot, cold or even re-heated.

JERUSALEM ARTICHOKES PROVENÇALE

Jerusalem artichokes look like potatoes with knobs on. Don't let this slightly strange arrangement put you off, they have a lovely, delicious hazelnut flavour. The real problem comes if you decide to try and peel them – avoid any recipe that requires it! Serve this as a separate course on its own or, if you feel like a light supper, a couple of fried eggs served on top is traditional and extremely delicious. You need some bread to help mop up the juice afterwards.

Attachments
slicing disc
double-bladed knife

Ingredients
1 lb (450 g) Jerusalem artichokes
1 large onion
2 cloves garlic
7 oz (195 g) tin Italian tomatoes
1 oz (25 g) butter
1 tablespoon oil
½ teaspoon each, sweet basil and oregano
salt and pepper

Method
Wash the artichokes and cut off any outrageously shaped bits or pieces that are discoloured. Pack them into the feed-tube and slice them, then rinse in a colander. Melt the oil and butter in a large thick frying pan and, when it's foaming, add the artichoke slices in an even layer. Give them a shake and turn the heat down. Meanwhile, without washing out the bowl, change the slicing disc for the double-bladed knife and add the peeled, quartered onion, the peeled garlic and the tin of tomatoes. Process for 10 seconds until fairly smooth. Turn the artichokes over with a fish slice, add the onion and tomato mixture and simmer for about 30 minutes until the liquid has almost dried up, a thick jammy sauce is left, and the artichokes are soft. Sprinkle the vegetables with the herbs, salt and pepper, and serve either in the frying pan or in a white china dish where the rich colours of the sauce are shown off best.

CARROTS VICHY

The people of Vichy believe the famous spa water is perfect for cooking carrots. Only the French, I think, would go to the trouble of specifying a particular sort of water, but they certainly do have the right technique. This produces lovely buttery, slightly candied carrots which are an absolute pleasure. Make sure you make twice as many as you think you need for that's how many people will eat.

Attachment
slicing disc

Ingredients
2 lb (900 g) carrots
1½ oz (40 g) butter
1 tablespoon sugar
pinch of salt

Method
Peel the carrots, pack them vertically into the feed-tube and slice them a batch at a time. Melt the butter in a wide saucepan and, having turned the carrot slices in it quickly, add a pinch of salt, enough water to barely cover them, and finish by sprinkling on the sugar. Bring to the boil and cook for about 12 minutes. They are ready when all the water has been absorbed and a gentle sizzle is heard from the carrots just starting to fry in the butter. They may need a little more salt at this stage. They should be eaten while they are really piping hot.

Mixed Fried Vegetables

This dish has three special advantages. The first is that it's very simple to do, especially using the slicing disc, secondly it looks really pretty, and thirdly it can be ready just five minutes after you've started – a great boon for unexpected guests or a quick snack before going out. Once again it uses the basic Chinese technique of stir-frying. The combination of vegetables is both pretty and unexpected, so it's a pity to use it only when you're having fried rice.

Attachments
slicing disc
grating disc

Ingredients
2 green peppers
2 carrots
1 onion
½ lb (225 g) bean sprouts or ½ lb (225 g) cabbage, shredded in the processor
2 tablespoons oil
salt and pepper

Method
Halve and de-seed the green peppers. Peel and cut the onion in half, and peel the carrots. Put the green peppers, packed tightly together into the feed-tube, slice them and then slice the onion. If you're using cabbage and not bean sprouts, slice this at the same time. Change the slicing disc for the grating disc and pack the carrots lengthwise into the feed-tube then switch on and grate them into the mixture. Grating them lengthwise will produce long, thin slivers of carrot. Heat 2 tablespoons of oil in a deep frying pan and add all the vegetables. Toss them swiftly for about a minute and cover for one minute more over a low heat. Raise the heat again, season generously and toss once more. You can add a teaspoon each of lemon juice and sugar, or a tablespoon of soy sauce and a teaspoon of butter at this stage. Both are delicious but I quite like the mixture on its own with the clear, clean taste of the vegetables brought out by the high-speed cooking and the simple seasoning.

1&2 Slice the peppers, followed by the onion and cabbage (if using), by packing them tightly together into the feed-tube.

3 Grate the carrots into the mixture, placing them lengthwise into the feed-tube.

4 Heat the oil in a deep frying pan and add all the vegetables.

FOR THAT ORIENTAL TOUCH EAT YOUR MIXED FRIED VEGETABLES WITH CHOPSTICKS.

BROCCOLI WITH OYSTER SAUCE

You can buy oyster sauce in any supermarket these days but it is worth looking at the label quite closely to make sure that it really contains oysters and isn't just soy sauce with a specially-devised flavouring. It is traditional to use this very delicate and not very fishy tasting sauce with lightly cooked green vegetables to give them an added richness and I like it particularly with broccoli. Broccoli cooked this way, by the way, is a revelation if you are just used to the bright green frozen kind – it has got terrific texture as well as flavour and makes an interesting accompaniment to non-Chinese dishes as well.

Attachment
thin slicing disc

Ingredients
*1 lb (450 g) fresh broccoli
1 clove garlic
1 inch (2.5 cm) fresh ginger
2 tablespoons oil
4 tablespoons oyster sauce
½ teaspoon salt*

Method
Cut the heads off the broccoli. Trim the stalks and pack into the feed-tube. Slice as thinly as possible and set aside. Crush the garlic and chop it and the peeled ginger finely (you can do this in the processor if you wish). Heat the oil in a wok or a big frying pan and fry the garlic and ginger for 1 minute, being careful that they don't burn. Add the sliced broccoli stalks and fry for 2 minutes more, turning them gently. Finally add the heads, broken into even sized pieces, turn them in the oil and add 4 tablespoons of water, keeping the heat high so that the broccoli steams as well as fries. When it is bright green and cooked through but still crunchy, season with the salt and put into a serving dish. Pour the oyster sauce over the hot broccoli and give it a turn to make sure it is well coated. Save a little sauce to pour just over the top as a final dressing before serving.

MANGE-TOUT STIR-FRY

The Chinese call mange-tout ('eat-all') snow peas. The vegetables in this recipe may seem a little exotic but the peas are widely available now, and big white radish, or mouli as it is variously known, is also easily found in a lot of supermarkets and most speciality Asian or Indian stores. I am not quite sure why, but this delicious trio of vegetables makes one of the nicest and simplest of all stir-fry dishes.

Attachment
thin slicing disc

Ingredients
*8 oz (225 g) each of mange-tout or sugar snap peas, mouli or large white radish
1 red pepper
1 tablespoon oil
2 tablespoons light soy sauce
salt*

Method
Trim and string the peas, split the red pepper and remove the seeds, peel the radish and cut into 2 inch lengths. Put the radish horizontally into the feed-tube and slice thinly. Slice the red pepper halves equally thinly. Heat the oil in a frying pan or wok until it is very hot, add the peas and stir for 1 minute. Add the radish and stir for another minute. Put the red peppers in, turn the heat down and cook together for 3 minutes. Season lightly with a little salt and add the light soy sauce, tossing the vegetables in it and serve immediately. The colour combination of red, white and green is most appealing.

CHILLI GINGER CABBAGE

Chinese cabbage (or Chinese leaves, as they are known) is a vegetable that has recently become widely available in Britain. It looks like a very light green Cos lettuce and can be eaten either as a salad, see page 46, or cooked very quickly using the stir-fry method. The flavourings come from Szechwan, in the western end of China, and have a rather unusual bite to them – with no trace of soy sauce.

Attachment
slicing disc

Ingredients
1 lb (450 g) Chinese cabbage
1 onion
1 inch (2.5 cm) long piece of fresh ginger
1/2 teaspoon chilli powder
1 oz (25 g) butter
1 dessertspoon brown sugar
1/2 cup water
3 tablespoons oil
salt

Method
Take off any discoloured leaves from the cabbage and cut it lengthwise into quarters. Press it in the feed-tube with the slicing disc in position and slice it quarter by quarter. Put aside and then slice the onion. Peel the ginger root, chop it finely. Heat the oil in a large frying pan, add the ginger and let it sizzle for about 30 seconds, add the onions and turn them, and then add the cabbage pieces. Turn rapidly for about a minute and half making sure they all get coated with the ginger-flavoured oil, and are heated through thoroughly. Add the butter, the brown sugar, the water and a good teaspoon of salt. Cook over a very high heat for another 1–1½ minutes. Cover and leave for 1 minute more. Remove the cover, turn the heat back up to high, sprinkle on the chilli powder, toss rapidly for 30 seconds and serve in a heated bowl with all the juices poured over. If you don't like your food too spicy, cut down on the chilli.

POTATO GALETTE

This is a kind of potato pie, with a crisp brown exterior and the potatoes making their own creamy buttery filling. It can be cooked in a pan on the top of a stove, or in the oven. Either way the secret of the whole dish is the super thin slicing that the processor does so effortlessly, and the careful washing of the potatoes before you cook them.

Attachment
slicing disc

Ingredients
2 lb (900 g) potatoes (preferably the waxy kind)
2 oz (50 g) butter
2 oz (50 g) cooking oil
salt and pepper
sliver of garlic

Method
Wash and peel the potatoes, trim them to fit the feed-tube and slice into the bowl. Empty the potato slices into a pan of clean cold water and swish them around until all the starch has been washed off and the water is quite cloudy, then drain. Heat a frying pan or a flat oven-proof dish and put ⅔ of the oil and butter into it, let it sizzle and quickly, before it burns (having taken it off the heat. Layer the potato slices around it in an even pattern building it up so that it forms a thick potato pancake. Press it down with a spatula – not your hand because steam will come sizzling out – and either turn the heat on the stove down, or place the dish in the oven to bake. In either case, do not cover. Leave for 15 minutes. Put a plate over the pan, and holding very carefully, turn upside down so the galette falls onto the plate. Melt the rest of the butter and oil, and swirl the garlic round the pan. Carefully slide the galette, cooked side uppermost, back into the pan, and cook for a further 20 minutes. When ready, both sides should be crispy brown, but with the centre creamy and delicious, with a flavour of the butter and garlic. Season, and serve cut in wedges rather like a cake.

POMMES DAUPHINOISE

Just to prove they haven't run out of ideas with sliced potatoes the French have another dish using the same basic ingredients but tasting completely different. This one comes from the eastern edge of France where the weather can get pretty nippy in the winter. It's a lovely warming, filling dish and incredibly rich. If you happen to have any dieters about don't serve it because it can break down the most determined resolve. It has another advantage, not common in potato dishes, in that it won't spoil if kept waiting and can safely be left in the oven for an extra half hour or so without coming to any harm.

Attachment
slicing disc

Ingredients
1½ lb (675 g) waxy potatoes
1 clove garlic
2 oz (50 g) butter
½ pint (300 ml) creamy milk
salt and pepper

Method
Peel the potatoes and slice finely using the slicing disc and then rinse them in a bowl of clean cold water until all the starch is washed off. Take a deep earthenware casserole and rub it carefully with a cut clove of garlic (you can add more if you like). Smear the inside of the dish with a little of the butter and then layer the potatoes into it, until you have used them all up. Every inch or so dot in some knobs of butter and sprinkle salt and pepper over them. Pour in the milk, add another few dots of butter and some salt and pepper, cover and put in a 350°F, 175°C, gas mark 4 oven to bake for 1 hour. Take the lid off and leave for another 20 minutes for it to form a crisp crust. At this stage you can turn the oven down, cover the dish and leave it for up to another 45 minutes without spoiling. The garlic, butter and milk combine deliciously with the potatoes to produce a dish with a delicate and unexpectedly rich flavour. Traditionally this is served with roast lamb, and I must say I don't think I've ever found a better partner for it.

1 **Finely slice the potatoes and wash off all the starch.**

2 **Rub a casserole with a cut clove of garlic, and then smear with a little butter.**

3 Layer the potatoes, dotting in knobs of butter and then sprinkle salt and pepper over them.

4 Pour in the milk, and add a few more dots of butter and salt and pepper.

DIETERS BEWARE! POMMES DAUPHINOISE CAN BREAK DOWN THE MOST DETERMINED RESOLVE.

SPROUT PURÉE

That much under-rated vegetable the Brussels sprout is almost uneatable late in the season. This recipe comes to the rescue – it's so delicious that I even make it when I can buy the hard, crisp, nutty sprouts left by early frosts. Once again, incredibly hard work without a processor but merely a whisk away with your friendly kitchen aid. Don't skimp on the butter or black pepper in this recipe, they really do make a colossal difference.

Attachment
double-bladed knife

Ingredients
1½ lb (675 g) Brussels sprouts
2 oz (50 g) butter
1 dessertspoon of freshly ground black pepper
1 tablespoon of lemon juice
salt

Method
Clean the sprouts, discarding the discoloured leaves. Put them in a pan of boiling water and cook for about 7 minutes, which will leave them still bright green but cooked through. Drain thoroughly and process them for 10 seconds. Scrape down the sides and process again until a fairly smooth purée is achieved. Add the butter, lemon juice, a good pinch of salt and the black pepper and process until thoroughly mixed. Pile into a white china serving bowl. It's absolutely delicious as an accompaniment to almost all roast meat dishes.

PUNCHEP

This is really a rustic, vegetable dish from my Welsh childhood, but with a processor it is turned into something more delicate. If you like your food a touch rustic process for a little bit less time than I recommend and you'll get the grainy texture that I remember so well from my youth.

Attachment
double-bladed knife

Ingredients
1 lb (450 g) carrots
1 lb (450 g) yellow swedes
2 oz (50 g) butter
black pepper
salt

Method
Peel the carrots and swedes and cut them into large dice, about an inch across. Boil them in lightly salted water for about 15 minutes until they are thoroughly cooked, but not falling apart. Drain and leave them to stand in the colander for about 3 minutes to remove any surplus liquid. Place them in the bowl and process for 10 seconds. Add the butter, scrape down the sides, season with salt and plenty of black pepper and process again until the mixture is smooth and fluffy.

PEA AND LETTUCE PURÉE

The combination of lettuce, peas and onions is an ancient one, probably brought to France by the Italian cooks who arrived in the late middle ages to introduce the pea to the phlegmatic northerners. This is my own version, particularly useful with some of the fresh peas you buy these days which seem to lack the sweetness and tenderness of those I remember some years ago. There are rumours that this is because all the good ones have been frozen. It is possible to make the dish with frozen peas if you like, reducing the cooking time from 15 to 5 minutes.

Attachment
double-bladed knife

Ingredients
1 lb (450 g) peas, fresh, podded or frozen
½ lettuce heart
6 spring onions
2 oz (50 g) butter
salt and pepper

Method
Cook the peas with the lettuce heart which you have shredded and the spring onions which you have sliced finely for the appropriate length of time, 15 minutes for fresh, 5 minutes for frozen. You can add a pinch of sugar to the water in either case if you think the peas may not be sweet enough, but don't salt them until they finish cooking as this tends to make them too hard. When the mixture is cooked, drain it, put it in the processor and add the butter which you have melted in the pan in which the peas were cooked. Process in 3 or 4 bursts of about 5 seconds, scraping the sides down so the mixture is really smooth. It should still be a pretty, bright green; season it now with salt and pepper and serve it in individual soufflé type dishes or cups. It has a wonderful, delicate flavour which can be used either on its own with fried or toasted bread triangles or to accompany light dishes such as chicken or fish.

SPINACH À LA CRÈME

Back to France for this dish, where I'm afraid, as is only too often the case, they know how to make the best of the vegetables that we grow so well but tend to under-use. If spinach has always made you feel that it was best left to Popeye, I do urge you to try this dish, just once. It could change your life because the combination of flavour and texture is something that only specialist chefs can normally achieve. I'm extremely fond of this dish eaten on its own, with triangles of bread fried in butter, the crispness of the butter-fried bread and the creamy delicate green of the spinach is sensational. It's also a good vegetable to go with one of your special fish or chicken dishes. Do take the trouble to buy fresh spinach – frozen spinach can be cooked like this, but just doesn't have the same strength of flavour, or vibrant colour.

Attachment
double-bladed knife

Ingredients
2 lb (900 g) spinach
3 fl oz (90 ml) double cream
2 oz (50 g) butter
black pepper
salt

Method
Wash the spinach carefully and trim off any thick stalks. Place it in a large saucepan without any water except that which is left on it from washing. Cover it with a lid and put it over a high heat for about 3 minutes. Take off the lid, stir and cook it with the lid off until it dries out (surprisingly, spinach cooked like this will produce more liquid than you would believe). It should be cooked in about 5 minutes. When the liquid is almost gone add the butter and toss with the spinach until the butter has melted and the spinach is properly coated. Put the cream into a separate pan, and heat it gently. Put the spinach into the bowl and process for 5 seconds, scrape down the sides, process again for another 5 seconds and with the motor running, pour in the very hot (just below boiling point) cream. Do not be tempted to use more than a small carton otherwise the dish will become too runny. Season with salt and black pepper. I'm quite fond of a little grated nutmeg with this dish as well, for it seems to bring out the flavour of the spinach and butter particularly nicely.

STIR-TOSSED COURGETTES

Courgettes can be eaten raw in salad as readily as cucumber. This dish doesn't leave them raw but cooks them at an incredible speed – do trust me on timings even though they seem unlikely. Courgettes for this recipe, by the way, don't need to be sliced and sorted as some recipe books recommend.

Attachment
medium or thin slicing disc

Ingredients
1 lb (450g) courgettes
2 tablespoons olive oil
1 teaspoon garlic salt
1 tablespoon thick tomato purée

Method
Trim, top and tail the courgettes and slice them on the slicing disc. Heat the oil in a large frying pan or saucepan, put in the courgettes, put the lid on and shake vigorously over a high heat for 30 seconds. Take the lid off, add the tomato purée and the level teaspoon of garlic salt, put the lid back on, and shake the pan again. Leave for 45 seconds, shake again and serve. The courgettes will be hot, garlicky, covered in tomato, still crunchy and absolutely delicious.

BUTTERED MUSHROOMS

Attachment
medium or thin slicing disc

Ingredients
1½ lb (675 g) button mushrooms
3 oz (75 g) butter
4 tablespoons chopped parsley
½ clove garlic
salt and pepper

Method
Rinse the trimmed, unpeeled button mushrooms under hot or boiling water in a sieve. Set them aside to drain for a moment. Put a medium, or, if you have no choice, a thin slicing blade into the processor, pack the mushrooms into the feed tube and slice gently. Heat 2 oz (50 g) of the butter with the crushed ½ clove of garlic for 2 minutes. When the butter stops sizzling, remove the garlic and add the mushrooms, turning thoroughly until coated with the butter. Cover the pan and shake over a high heat for about a minute until the mushrooms are heated right through, but not soggy. Add the finely chopped parsley, stir, and pile onto a plate. Heat the remaining butter in the pan until it foams and pour over the mushrooms. Season and serve immediately.

STIR-TOSSED COURGETTES – CRUNCHY AND DELICIOUS.

Perfect Pastry

The secret of good pastry is how much you handle it. The less, the better, because coolness and speed, whatever the method, are essential. This is where a processor comes into its own – it rubs in and mixes in seconds, and as it's untouched by human hands the pastry stays cool, calm and controllable in a way that only the very best pastry chefs can achieve.

I have suggested four different kinds of pastry in this chapter for different sorts of things. For the French-style open tarts, full of highly flavoured ingredients in a delicate creamy sauce, I suggest the crisp French *brisée* pastry. For the rather more solid recipes from the English counties like game pie or apple pie, I use a more traditional English shortcrust. But my favourites are delicious crisp biscuity shells filled with fresh summer fruits – strawberries, raspberries, cherries, coated in a gleaming glaze and looking almost too attractive to eat. To make those you need the French *sablé* pastry. Lastly, for the truly adventurous, choux pastry, the stuff that éclairs are made of and cooks' reputations shattered by, unless you

happen to have a processor in your kitchen. With all these pastries, the amazing processor makes many of the most skilled and difficult parts of the work effortless, and also speeds up the whole process quite remarkably.

As someone who's not a natural pastry maker, one of the things I've learned over the years is that confidence is very important. Get all the ingredients together, make sure you know what to do before you start, and then *do* it. Flat out, and without losing your nerve half way. It's amazing what a difference that particular style makes to any pastry making. Indeed, it's not a bad rule for cooking in general.

Don't skip the thirty minutes in the fridge I recommend for all the pastries. It makes sure that they hardly shrink when they are cooked, and it also makes them a great deal easier to handle when you are rolling or pressing out into the tins or dishes. Also, don't forget decoration: a little bit of pastry rolled out flat, cut in the shape of a leaf or two, and stuck on with a drop of water or egg adds the finishing touch.

Pâte Brisée

French Savoury Pastry

Pâte brisée is French savoury pastry. It's traditionally made as a container for the mixtures that make the huge variety of quiches and open pies that the French adore as first courses, or as a main course for a light meal. It's rather tougher than our shortcrust pastry and can be handled more firmly and used more thinly. The key to this extra strength is the egg yolk which goes into the pastry. Don't be tempted to leave it out. The quantities given are for one 8–10 inch (20–25 cm) open flan.

Attachment
double-bladed knife

Ingredients
5 oz (150 g) flour
2 oz (50 g) butter
1 egg yolk
½ teaspoon salt
1½–2 tablespoons cold water

Method
Put the flour, salt and roughly chopped butter into the bowl and process until the mixture resembles very coarse breadcrumbs (about 5 seconds). Add the egg yolk and water and process until the mixture starts to ball up around the knife. Switch off and empty the pastry onto a floured board. Gather it all together and knead it two or three times with the heel of your hand until it forms a firm ball, wrap it in foil or cling film and put it in the fridge. It should be left for at least 30 minutes, up to a couple of hours won't hurt. When you're ready to use it, you can either roll it out on a floured board in the normal manner or press it into the tin with the knuckles of your hand which is my favourite method. Put it into a hot oven, 400°F, 200°C, gas mark 6, whether you're baking it empty (blind) or with a filling. If you're baking blind make sure you've put in a piece of foil weighed down with some beans or rice to stop the pastry base puffing up in the sudden strong heat. If empty it should be baked for about 10 minutes.

1 **Process the flour, salt and roughly chopped butter until they resemble very coarse breadcrumbs.**

2 **Add the egg yolk to the mixture.**

3 **Add the water.**

4 **Process the mixture.**

5 **Stop when the mixture starts to ball up around the knife, and empty onto a floured board.**

6 **Knead the pastry two or three times with the heel of your hand.**

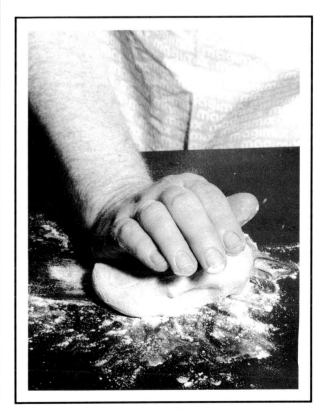

Onion Quiche

This is a recipe for one of the simplest of all quiches. It is both creamy and flavourful, and although there are a lot of onions, it hasn't got the kind of afterglow that makes you 'not nice-to-know'. It has the other advantage of being made with the sort of ingredients you usually have in the house. It is important to cook the onions before putting them into the quiche, and you can add a clove of garlic, also sliced very finely if you like.

Attachments
slicing disc
double-bladed knife

Ingredients
1 lb (450 g) onions
1 tablespoon butter
2 eggs
1 egg yolk
7 fl oz (220 ml) milk
grated nutmeg
salt and pepper
a recipe pâté brisée

1 **Finely slice the peeled onions.**

Method

Peel the onions and slice them finely through the slicing disc. Turn them gently in the butter for about 5 minutes until they are soft but not brown. Line a 8–10 inch (20–25 cm) flan dish with the pastry and spread the onion mixture onto that. Change to the double-bladed knife and process the eggs, egg yolk, milk and seasonings together. Pour the egg mixture gently into the flan – it should come to not less than $\frac{1}{2}$ inch from the top to prevent if from spilling over as it rises. Bake at 425°F, 220°C, gas mark 7, for 25 minutes; turn down to 375°F, 190°C, gas mark 5, for another 5–10 minutes until the top is well browned and the pastry cooked through. Serve this hot or cold, but remember it will sink a little as it cools.

2 **Place them in a pan, turning in the butter for about 5 minutes, until soft.**

3 Spread the onion mixture onto the pastry-lined flan dish.

4 Process the eggs, egg yolk, milk and seasoning.

5 Pour the egg mixture carefully into the flan.

ONION QUICHE – SIMPLE BUT DELICIOUS.

CHEESE QUICHE

The most popular quiche in France is almost certainly the one made from Gruyère cheese, the very rich cheese made in Switzerland, France (and probably nowadays in Ireland and Italy as well), which adds a distinctive flavour to French cooking. You can use very mature Cheddar or Leicester cheese, but whatever else you do, don't use any of the processed types of cheese as they simply won't blend in when they're cooked. Cheese quiche is also one of those dishes to which you can add your own bits; a few mushrooms, a few spears of asparagus, some left-over cooked mixed vegetables can all be added and will enhance the quiche as long as you don't overdo it.

Attachments
grating disc
double-bladed knife

Ingredients
1 recipe pâté brisée
8 oz (225 g) Gruyère (or Leicester or Cheddar) cheese
2 eggs
1 egg yolk
7 fl oz (220 ml) milk
1 dessertspoon cornflour
salt and pepper

Method
Line an 8–9 inch (20–22.5 cm) flan tin with pastry. Grate the cheese, take it out of the bowl, put in the double-bladed knife, add the cornflour, milk, eggs and seasonings, and process until smooth. Mix half the cheese into this mixture, and pour it into the pastry case. Season and sprinkle the rest of the cheese over the egg mixture. Make sure it does not come to within half an inch from the top, otherwise, as the pie cooks, the mixture, which rises quite a lot, will spill over the sides. Bake it at 425°F, 220°C, gas mark 7 for 25–20 minutes. It's best eaten hot, as the risen pie sinks as it cools.

QUICHE PROVENÇALE

This pie is really a bit of a crafty cheat because the pastry is cooked in advance and the filling is really poured in and just heated up in the pastry rather than cooked with the raw shell. It's delicious, however, and again is one of those adaptable recipes that can bend to the availability of ingredients. One thing, do not be tempted to use bottled pimento olives, because the vinegar and extra salt in the preserving liquid will make the pastry soggy.

Attachment
slicing disc

Ingredients
1 recipe pâté brisée
1 recipe ratatouille (page 78)
1 oz (25 g) black olives
1 teaspoon each basil and oregano

Method
Line an 8 inch (20 cm) flan tin with the pastry, then line it with a piece of foil and weight it down with a handful of rice or dried beans. Bake it at 400°F, 200°C, gas mark 6 for 10 minutes. Take the foil and beans out, bake for a further 5 minutes, then leave it to cool. You can use either left-over ratatouille or make it fresh. Either way, fill the pie shell with warm, but not hot, ratatouille. Place the olives in an attractive pattern across the top, sprinkle with the mixed herbs and salt and pepper if the vegetables are not already highly seasoned. Put back in the oven for not more than 10–15 minutes, until the vegetable mixture is heated right through. When you're putting the ratatouille in it's a good trick to do so with a slotted spoon to drain off any extra juice.

SHORTCRUST PASTRY

BRITISH SAVOURY PASTRY

If you have a favourite shortcrust pastry recipe, try making it in the processor, rubbing the flour and fat in together first and adding the liquid afterwards. My own experience is that any recipe I'm used to making by hand probably needs a little more flour added to it when using a processor, as the blending and mixing is rather more thorough than you can achieve by hand. Don't add much water at first but add it bit by bit or the pastry will suddenly ball up around the knife. If you haven't got a favourite short-crust recipe try using this one.

Attachment
double-bladed knife

Ingredients
6 oz (175 g) plain flour
2 oz (50 g) butter
2–3 tablespoons water
pinch salt

Method
Put the butter, cut into two or three chunks, into the bowl with the flour and salt. Process until it resembles fairly coarse breadcrumbs. This takes about 5–10 seconds (you may need to scrape the sides of the bowl down once during the process). Then, with the motor running, add the water, a tablespoonful at a time. Flours vary with the amount of water they can absorb, so you'll have to check as you go. When the pastry is made, it will suddenly form a ball around the knife and at this point switch off. Scrape out the bowl thoroughly, and very gently press all the pastry pieces together into one solid lump. Wrap it in foil or cling film, put it in the fridge for about half an hour.

GAME PIE

Traditionally, game pies were made with 'hot water' pastry, and decorated with extravagant shapes. The traditional Grosvenor Pie is probably the last remnant of this type of cooking. I think that a delicious game pie can be made using shortcrust pastry and the one or two cheaper forms of game that are still available. This pie is intended to be served hot, but if you want to serve it cold, proceed as below but make it in a loaf tin rather than an oval pie dish. This will make slicing easier, and before it cools use a funnel to pour some melted jellied consommé through the slits in the top until it fills the pie up completely. It feeds 6 easily.

Attachment
double-bladed knife

Ingredients
1 recipe shortcrust pastry
2 lb (900 g) game (either back legs and saddle of a hare, or 4 or 5 pigeons or stewing venison)
8 oz (225 g) onions
2 tablespoons dripping or oil
2 tablespoons flour
4 oz (100 g) button mushrooms
4 tablespoons redcurrant jelly
2 bay leaves
½ teaspoon dried thyme
½ teaspoon dried marjoram
salt and pepper

Method
Put the cleaned game in a saucepan and cover with water. Make sure there's at least an inch over the top. Bring to the boil, skim off any scum and simmer for 30 minutes. Remove the stalks from the mushrooms and add them with the peeled and quartered onions to the processor. Process until finely chopped, and then fry in the dripping or oil for 5 or 6 minutes. Sprinkle with flour and stir until smooth. Add 3 cups of the stock in which the game was cooked and make a smooth sauce. Remove the meat from the bones, cut into neat chunks and add to the sauce with the redcurrant jelly and herbs, and season generously. Line a deep (1½ inch) pie dish and with half the pastry put in the game mixture, put the button mushroom caps along the top and cover with the remaining pastry rolled out thinly. Trim the edges, brush the pie with egg beaten up with a little milk, and make two deep slits in the centre for the steam to escape. Bake it in a medium oven, 375°F, 190°C, gas mark 5 for 45 minutes covering with a little foil if the top starts to brown before the rest of the pie is cooked.

1 **Slicing the carrots and leeks.**

2 **Pouring the thickened stock over the dish.**

CHICKEN PIE

A lovely farmhouse-style recipe, made, if you can get one, with the cheaper, and slightly more tasty boiling fowl. The stock from cooking the chicken makes a wonderful basis for a soup.

Attachment
slicing disc

Ingredients
1 recipe shortcrust pastry
3 lb (1.3 kg) boiling fowl (or roasting chicken)
8 oz (225 g) carrots
1 lb (450 g) leeks
4 oz (100 g) button mushrooms
bay leaf
large piece parsley stalk
2 hard-boiled eggs
1 tablespoon cornflour
1 tablespoon chopped parsley
salt and pepper

Method
Put the chicken and the washed giblets into a saucepan big enough to hold them comfortably. Pour over water to come at least 2 inches above the chicken, bring to the boil and skim off any scum. Meanwhile, peel the carrots and clean the leeks thoroughly in running water, stripping any discoloured outer leaves. Slice the carrots and the leeks through the

3 **Adding the finishing touch.**

slicing disc and add them to the skimmed chicken pot. Add the bay leaf and parsley stalk and simmer until the chicken is tender. This may be for as little as 30 minutes for a roasting chick, 1¼ hours for a boiling fowl. Keep the lid on and don't season with salt or pepper at this stage. Wash the button mushrooms thoroughly and if they're large, cut them in half. Peel the hard-boiled eggs and cut them in half. When the chicken is cooked, remove it and the vegetables from the stock, skin it and take the meat off the bones. (You can put the skin and bones back into the stock to enrich it.) Mix 2 ladlesful of the stock with the cornflour and whisk thoroughly. Mix the chicken pieces and the cooked vegetables together and fill an oval pie dish almost to the brim. Season it at this stage, add the chopped parsley and pour over the stock and cornflour. Lay the hard-boiled eggs, cut side up, on top and press gently so that they're barely covered by the sauce. Take a

quarter of the pastry and roll it into a long thin sausage-like shape which will fit around the rim of the dish. Moisten the edge with cold water and carefully press the pastry roll on top of it. Roll out the remaining pastry so that it fits the shape of the dish, moisten the pastry on the edge of the dish with cold water again, and lay the sheet of pastry over the top of it. Using the back of a fork, mark it all the way round pressing the sheet of pastry into the sausage-shape around the edge of the dish. Trim the excess off with a knife and use it to make decorations to put on the centre of the pie. Cut a hole in the middle and bake the whole dish at 425°F, 220°C, gas mark 7 for 25 minutes until the pastry is nicely browned on top. You can, if you like, glaze the pastry with a little milk or beaten egg, before putting it into the oven. This produces a lovely shiny appearance. The chicken pie can be eaten hot or cold.

CHICKEN PIE CAN BE EATEN HOT OR COLD – DELICIOUS EITHER WAY

ENGLISH APPLE PIE

There is as much dispute about what makes a good English apple pie as there are cooks who cook it. However, most people seem to agree on a single crust, thinly sliced apples and not too much spicing. The only addition to this can be a flavouring of quince, that unusual fruit which tends only to be used for jellies or jams.

Attachment
slicing disc

Ingredients
1 recipe sweet shortcrust pastry
1¹/₂ lb (675 g) cooking apples
6 oz (175 g) sugar
2 tablespoons quince jelly or marmalade (optional)
grated rind of a lemon
pinch of allspice

Method
Peel, core and halve the apples and slice them through the slicing disc. Grease an 8 inch (20 cm) pie dish and put in the apples sprinkling them with sugar and the lemon rind as you go. If you are using it spread the quince jelly or marmalade on the top and add the pinch of allspice. Pile the apples up in the centre so that they form a peak that is at least ¹/₂ inch above the edge of the dish. This is because the apples will almost certainly sink as they cook and the pie will otherwise have a dent in the middle. Roll the pastry out, damp the edges of the plate, place the pastry on the top, trim the edges off and decorate the circumference with the back of a fork. Cut a double slot in the middle and bake at 400°F, 200°C, gas mark 6 for 35 minutes. Turn the oven down to 350°F, 180°C, gas mark 4, and bake for a further 10 minutes, putting a little foil over the pastry if it's browning too quickly. You can serve this pie hot or cold. If you let it get cold it'll sink a little bit from its high point in the centre. At the point where you turn the oven down, you can, if you like, sprinkle the top with a little caster sugar which produces a nice glazed, slightly crunchy appearance.

AMERICAN APPLE PIE

Another deep dish pie but one with a very different flavour and texture when it's cooked. It's very often eaten in America hot out of the oven, with a large dollop of vanilla ice cream, and is known as *pie-à-la-mode*. Even if you eat it cold, it's still very nice with thick cream or ice-cream ladled on top of it.

Attachment
double-bladed knife

Ingredients
1¹/₂ lb (675 g) eating apples (the Americans don't have cookers)
1 tablespoon cornflour
1 tablespoon lemon juice
6 oz (175 g) sugar
1 teaspoon each ground cinnamon and cloves
1 recipe shortcrust pastry
1 oz (25 g) butter

Method
Put the peeled cored apples cut in quarters into the bowl with the cornflour and lemon juice and process briefly until the apples are still in chunks but chopped down quite a lot, and the cornflour and lemon juice have been mixed all over them. Line a deep pie dish with half the pastry, pile in the apple mixture, seasoning it with the sugar and the mixed spices. Make sure it's piled at least an inch higher than the edge of the dish in the middle to prevent the pie sinking in the middle when it's cooked. Dot the surface of the apples with butter and cover with the second layer of pastry, wetting the rim first to make sure it will stick. Brush the top with a little milk or beaten egg if you want to glaze, cut two slots in the centre and bake at 400°F, 200°C, gas mark 6 for 40 minutes. Turn the oven off and leave the pie to cook in the remaining heat for another 5 minutes. It's usually served hot, but is equally delicious cold, in which case it is best to let it cool all the way down in the oven.

Pâté Sablé

The French version of sweet pastry is called *sablé,* which is the word for sand, because it is so crisp and sugary that when eaten it just crumbles away. It is not dry or gritty, but has a very soft texture. The inclusion of egg makes it surprisingly strong and water resistant. In parts of France they don't put anything in it at all, but roll it out flat, and cut it with biscuit cutters and make buttery biscuits called sablés, sometimes covered with a few slivered almonds.

Attachment
double-bladed knife

Ingredients
4 oz (100 g) flour
1½ tablespoons caster sugar
1 egg
2 oz (50 g) butter
pinch salt

Method
Put the flour, sugar, salt and butter, cut into chunks, into the bowl and process until the mixture resembles fine breadcrumbs. With the motor running, add the egg and stop the machine the moment it starts to form a ball. Tip it onto a floured board, press it all together with the heel of your hand, squash it flat a couple of times, knead it lightly, and roll it up into a ball. Wrap it in cling film and put it in the fridge for at least 30 minutes. After that, it's ready to be used. It won't suffer if it's kept tightly wrapped in a fridge for up to three days.

Crème Pâtissière

The most sumptuous part of French tarts for most foreigners is the fact that just beneath the fruit and before you get to the crisp pastry, there is a layer of what tastes like vanilla flavoured cream, known here as confectioner's cream. It is one of the easiest things in the world to make, and transforms an ordinary tart into something else! With a processor, of course, a lot of the art is already taken care of for you, so you can earn the praise without having to struggle.

Attachment
double-bladed knife

Ingredients
3 oz (75 g) caster sugar
2 eggs
2 oz (50 g) flour
¾ pint (450 ml) milk
½ teaspoon vanilla essence

Method
Put the eggs into the bowl, add the sugar and process until blended smoothly together. Add the flour and process again until mixed. Bring the milk to the boil and with the motor running, pour it carefully through the feed-tube into the bowl. Process for a further 5 seconds. Return to the saucepan, cook over a low heat for 5 minutes, stirring much of the time until the mixture thickens completely. Add the vanilla essence and leave it to cool, stirring occasionally to prevent a skin forming. It is now ready for use. It'll keep in the fridge for up to a week if it's covered, and is really one of the nicest and most sumptuous cheap luxuries I know.

PÂTÉ SABLÉ SHELLS CAN BE FILLED WITH CRÈME PÂTISSIÈRE AND FRESH FRUIT.

FRENCH FRUIT TART

Attachment
slicing disc

Ingredients
1 recipe pâté sablé
½ recipe crème pâtissière
2 lb (900 g) fruit – pears, peaches or plums
4 tablespoons apricot jam
4 tablespoons water

Method
Core or stone but don't peel the fruits, cut them in half and process them through the slicing disc. You'll probably need to stop and start the machine, packing the tube each time, to help to keep the slices even and tidy. Take an 8 inch (20 cm) flan tin, preferably one with a removable base, greased if it's not non-stick, and knuckle the pastry out across it until you have a pastry shell that comes about an ¹/₈ inch above the tin all the way round. Fill the centre with a piece of foil and rice or beans to weigh it down, and bake in the oven at 400°F, 200°C, gas mark 6 for 15 minutes. Take out the foil and let it bake for another 10 minutes. When the flan is cool fill it to within ¹/₂ inch of the top with the *crème pâtissière* which should also be cool but not chilled. Lay the fruit slices in circles around the pie so they form a scalloped, overlapping pattern. (If you have cut the fruit in advance, stand it in a little water and lemon juice to prevent it going brown.) Melt the apricot jam in the water until thoroughly mixed and, using a pastry brush or working with a spoonful at a time, spread the glaze over the fruit. Return the whole lot to the oven and cook for another 15–20 minutes making sure that the pastry doesn't burn at the edges. You can serve this hot if you like, but it is far nicer cooled down and allowed to set. If the fruit is a little burned on the top don't worry, it's the glaze caramelising and is totally authentic.

STRAWBERRY TART

One of the great joys in France in the strawberry season are the bakers' shops which appear to be absolutely inundated with tiny strawberry tarts. The pastry is gold and crumbly, the fruit uncooked, piled high in the tarts with an amazing shiny glaze that makes it look even more sumptuous and delicious. They can cost a small fortune, but are so easy to make at home that they are one of my favourite indulgences. One of the other virtues is that although best quality fruit is ideal you can use up end of season fruit which may not have quite the perfect shape and colour.

Ingredients
1 recipe of pâté sablé
½ recipe crème pâtissière
1 lb (450 g) strawberries
8 oz (225 g) strawberry jam
4 tablespoons water
1 tablespoon lemon juice

Method
Line a series of mini tart tins with the pâté sablé. Put a little crumpled foil in each one to prevent them going out of shape when you bake them and bake at 400°F, 200°C, gas mark 6, for 7 minutes. Take out the foil and bake for another 5 minutes or so, making sure none of the pastry starts to catch or burn. Take out of the oven, allow to cool and remove the pastry cases from the tin. Into the bottom of each one, put a couple of tablespoons of *crème pâtissière* and then pile in as many strawberries as it will conveniently and attractively hold. Do remember to keep a pretty strawberry for the top of the pile for each tart, as the decoration is one of the things that makes this look so sumptuous. Melt the strawberry jam with the water and lemon juice together in a saucepan and beat it until smooth, getting rid of as many of the lumps as possible. Take a tablespoonful and trickle over the top of each tart so that it runs down to the crevices between the strawberries, and make sure that none of the strawberries is left uncovered by the glaze. Allow to set and serve them when the whole confection is nice and cool. They are not greatly improved by being chilled in the fridge. I have been known to put a small dollop of whipped cream right on the top even though it may be a little like gilding the lily.

CHOUX PASTRY

Why this pastry is named after cabbages in France, I've never understood. It's the stuff that éclairs and whipped cream dreams are made of. I've only suggested three possible uses, because I think self-indulgence should have some limits, but if you've ever had a confection made with choux pastry you'd like to copy, this recipe will help you to do it effortlessly. Once again it's the processor that takes the hard work out of this professional pastry. This way, you wind up cool and refreshed, with all your energies available to devour the éclairs as soon as they're ready.

Attachment
double-bladed knife

Ingredients
2 oz (50 g) butter
8 fl oz (250 ml) water (just under ½ pint)
5 oz (150 g) flour
4 eggs

Method
Bring the water to the boil in a small saucepan, add the butter. Put the flour in the bowl, process for 2 or 3 seconds, and with the motor running pour the hot, boiling water and butter through the feed-tube. It should form an instant paste. Return it to the saucepan and, stirring, cook gently for 3 or 4 minutes. Put the mixture back into the bowl and, with the motor running, add the eggs one at a time through the feed-tube. The pastry should now be pale golden and like very sticky thick cream. Either take it up in tablespoons and place on a greased baking tray in dollops, in long sausage-shapes for éclairs, or use an icing bag with a ½ inch nozzle and pipe the shapes you want directly onto the tray. Either way, put the tray into a 425°F, 220°C, gas mark 7 oven and leave to cook for 25 minutes. The buns will rise so do make sure that you have left enough space for them. When they're cooked and golden brown, take them out of the oven and prick a hole with a skewer or a knife at the top of each to let the steam escape and keep the shell crisp and firm.

ÉCLAIRS

Ingredients
4 oz (100 g) bitter chocolate
1 oz (25 g) butter
1 fl oz (30 ml) water
1 tablespoon icing sugar
1 recipe choux pastry

Method
The long thin sausage-shapes are perfect for making éclairs. When they have cooled a little split them along one side carefully with a knife. Melt together the chocolate, butter, water and icing sugar and allow it to cool slightly before pouring carefully in a thin ribbon down each éclair. Spread it with a pallet knife which has been dipped in hot water so that it keeps the chocolate melted and smooth. If you have any chocolate left over, you can go back and put a second coating on, which is extremely greedy, but very delicious. When the chocolate is cool (do not put it in the fridge, let it cool in the kitchen), fill the centre of the éclairs either with *crème pâtissière* or whipped cream. *Crème pâtissière* will keep a little longer, but cream is perhaps a little more sumptuous.

PROFITEROLES

Perhaps one of the most widely enjoyed restaurant sweets in the world, profiteroles are really mini éclairs filled with whipped cream and with the chocolate coating still hot when they're eaten. They're a little trouble to prepare as they have to be done at the last minute, but well worth it for a grand case of showing off at a special dinner party.

Ingredients
1 recipe choux pastry
5 oz (150 g) double cream, whipped with
2 oz (50 g) caster sugar
4 oz (100 g) bitter chocolate
2 oz (50 g) butter
top of the milk from a pint of gold-top (Jersey)
grated rind of an orange

Method
Make the choux pastry and bake it on a greased baking tray as 24 tiny walnut sized balls. When these are cooked pierce the top with a skewer to let the steam out. When they're cool split each in half, and fill with the whipped cream. A dessertspoonful will go into each. Stack them into a shallow pyramid using a little of the cream as a kind of mortar and put aside. When you're ready to serve, melt the chocolate in the butter, add all the other ingredients and stir until thoroughly mixed smooth before quickly pouring it over the profiteroles. It is quite possibly one of the most fattening dishes in the entire world, and for its devotees, of whom I am one, well worth it.

SAVOURY PROFITEROLES

It is possible to make savoury profiteroles, choux buns or éclairs. They are delicious filled with something light and creamy like mackerel pâté, perhaps with a little fromage frais whipped into it to make it a lighter texture. For icing, if they are to be eaten immediately (preferably with a knife and fork), sour cream is fine. For longer term preparation, glaze the pastry as it finishes cooking with a beaten egg layered on 2 or 3 times at 1 minute intervals.

OPPOSITE: PROFITEROLES – PERHAPS ONE OF THE MOST WIDELY ENJOYED RESTAURANT SWEETS

PARIS-BREST CAKE

This is a famous French patisserie speciality. No one is quite sure why it is called after the two towns, maybe it was developed in one of the Inns between them in the days of the great coaching runs. It is surprisingly easy to make using the processor, but by hand it was quite an ordeal. It is a grand party piece looking good in the centre of a buffet table or to bring on at the end of a special dinner to a few oohs and aahs. It is, however, not for slimmers. With the best will in the world it is what can only be described as a rich self-indulgence, certainly to be enjoyed but perhaps in these days of more sensible eating, not too often.

Attachment
double-bladed knife

Ingredients (for 8)
1 recipe of choux pastry (page 102)
1 recipe of crème pâtissière (page 99)
4 oz (100 g) slivered almonds
3 oz (75 g) caster sugar
2 tablespoons icing sugar

Method
Divide the choux pastry up into 8 equal portions and put them in a ring on a greased baking sheet so that they just touch. As they rise they will blend together to make a complete ring. Bake according to the choux pastry instructions, 425°F, 220°C, gas mark 7 for about 20 minutes. Take out of the oven and allow to cool. Split the cake horizontally so you have two pieces, each like half a tyre. Tidy up the inside so that the bottom half makes a nice neat container for the filling. To make the filling, melt the sugar very gently in a non-stick saucepan and add the almonds. Allow to cook until a pale toffee-gold colour. Don't over-cook as the mixture burns very quickly. Pour it out onto a piece of oiled greaseproof paper and allow it to set. Put the double-bladed knife in the processor and when the mixture, which is called praline, is cold break it into large chunks and process until a fine powder. Stir this powder into the *crème pâtissière*, mixing it in thoroughly, and fill the cake with the mixture. Balance the top half on the filling, sprinkle through a sieve the 2 tablespoons of icing sugar and put it in the fridge to chill for at least 1 hour. When it is ready to serve you can decorate it with a few more slivered almonds that you have browned under the grill for a couple of minutes till they are coloured. Cut it in the sections effectively marked by the original 8 buns you baked and be sure to serve it to follow a light meal.

Beautiful Bread

Making bread with a processor is a real revelation. It's an amazing machine for a lot of cooking, but for bread-making it is revolutionary. It also produces bread that is actually better than any I have ever managed by hand, especially in terms of texture. This is because you get a fast thorough kneading of the dough that would require 15 to 20 minutes' hard, wrist-aching work by hand. As any baker's manual will tell you it's the kneading that makes the difference between average and really good bread. All these recipes will produce bread with a fine even textured crumb, and a well matured flavour, which makes it difficult to go back to shop bought bread at any time.

A couple of points about making bread at home. Buy the right kind of flour – if you are buying wholemeal make sure it's intended for bread-making and includes what is known as durum wheat, which helps to produce a firm, well-risen loaf. If you're buying white flour try and buy unbleached bread flour. It produces a perfectly white loaf, with a much richer flavour than the more ordinary commercial bleached varieties. If you can find it use wholemeal flour which has had only 15 per cent of the bran extracted. It produces what I think is probably the most delicious bread of all, well risen and as light as white bread, yet with a nuttiness and flavour of a good wholemeal.

One of the lovely things about making bread with a processor is that although it only takes you a couple of minutes' work, the lovely traditional processes that produce rich flavoured bread will look after themselves while you do something else. If you haven't got a couple of hours to let the bread rise properly you can always try the soda breads that I have suggested, equally delicious in their own right. Do give a try to one of the more unusual recipes, like the herb and onion bread, which is splendid eaten with farmhouse cheese, or as an accompaniment to a bowl of one of the richer soups on pages 15–24.

BROWN BREAD

This is made from flour which has had part of the bran extracted, but has enough left in it to give it both body and flavour, while allowing it to rise and produce the kind of texture that we are used to with white bread. It's sold marked 81 per cent or 85 per cent flour and most good supermarkets and almost all health food type stores stock it these days. I think it's the perfect compromise between wholemeal goodness and white bread luxury.

Attachment
double-bladed knife

Ingredients
12 oz (350 g) 81% or 85% flour
8 fl oz (250 ml) warm water
½ packet (1 teaspoon) instant dried yeast
1 teaspoon salt
1 tablespoon oil
1 tablespoon golden syrup

Method
Put the flour, yeast and salt into the bowl and add the golden syrup and the oil to the warm water. Process the flour and with the motor running add the golden syrup, oil and water mixture. Continue processing for about a minute then put the dough in a greased bowl and cover with cling-film. Leave it in a warm place for about an hour to an hour and a half when it should double in size. Knock it down, punching it until all the air comes out, put it back in the bowl, which doesn't need to have been washed, and process it for another 30 seconds. Take it out and shape it into a round about 6 inches across and domed in the middle. Cut a gash in the top with a sharp knife, and put it back in a warm place to rise for about 35 to 40 minutes, when it should again almost double in bulk. Put it into a preheated oven, 375°F, 190°C, gas mark 5, and turn the heat down to 350°F, 180°C, gas mark 4. It should take about 40 minutes to bake, giving off the most wheaty aroma towards the end but do not be tempted to undercook it because of the smell. Test it by lifting it up and tapping the bottom, which should sound hollow, a test for almost all bread. If it's ready, take it out and let it cool on a wire rack, if not give it another 5 or 10 minutes in the oven. This bread keeps marvellously and is delicious toasted.

WHITE BREAD

Compared to white bread you may have bought in the baker's, this is going to be a surprise. It will have a pale cream coloured crumb and a rich flavour that makes anything more than salty butter and the privacy of your own kitchen seem unnecessary. It improves with a day's keeping before eating it, so if you can stand it, don't let the marvellous baking smell make you tear it to pieces just after it comes out of the oven.

Attachment
double-bladed knife

Ingredients
12 oz (350 g) unbleached white bread flour
7 fl oz (200 ml) warm water
½ packet (1 teaspoon) instant dried yeast
1 teaspoon salt
1 tablespoon softened butter

Method
Put the flour, yeast, butter and salt into the bowl. Switch on and process for about 5 seconds. With the motor running pour the water in through the feed-tube. The dough will form a ball around the knife. Leave the machine on to thoroughly knead it for about a minute. Grease a bowl, take out the ball of dough, which should stick together, add any little bits that may have fallen off it, roll it in the oiled bowl, cover it with a piece of film and put it in a warm draught-free place – an airing cupboard is ideal – and leave to rise for about an hour. When it has doubled in size it's ready for the next process. Put it back in the bowl which need not have been washed in the meanwhile, knock it down, so all the air comes out (it's really rather like punching a pillow) put the cover on and process again for another 30 to 45 seconds. Take out and put in a ready greased 1 lb (450 g) loaf tin (or non-stick one, which I really think is even better). Put it back in a warm place, with a plastic cover over it if you like, and leave it until it's risen and has filled the tin. Preheat the oven 425°F, 220°C, gas mark 7. As soon as the bread has reached the top of the tin, place it in the oven and turn the heat down to 400°F, 200°C, gas mark 6. It should be ready in approximately 35 to 40 minutes, but you do need to test, because some ovens and some flours differ. Take the loaf out of the tin, and tap it on the bottom. If it sounds hollow, it's cooked. If not, leave it out of its tin, it doesn't need it to shape it any more, let it bake for another 10 minutes or so. When it is cooked take it out and cool it on a wire rack, or laid across the top of the tin so the air can circulate right the way round it.

OPPOSITE: TRADITIONAL FULL FLAVOURED BREADS WILL ONLY TAKE A FEW MINUTES OF YOUR TIME.

WHOLEMEAL BREAD

Traditionally wholemeal breads always seem difficult to make, and indeed only too often come out like leaden cake rather than proper bread. There is no way a real wholemeal is ever going to be as light or as delicately textured as white bread because the very ingredients that make it *whole*meal give it the bite and a solidity that has been removed from white flour. With a processor it is possible to have wholemeal bread with a lovely firm delicate texture, the kind that really does need to be eaten in large chunks with home-made chutneys and farmhouse cheeses. Don't be tempted to process this dough too long, wholemeal doesn't require anything like the kneading or processing that more refined flours need, and it's also meant to be a wetter dough.

Attachment
double-bladed knife

Ingredients
12 oz (350 g) wholemeal flour (make sure it's bread flour)
1 tablespoon black treacle
½ packet (1 teaspoon) instant dried yeast
8 fl oz (250 ml) warm water
1 tablespoon oil
1 teaspoon salt

Method
Put the flour, yeast and salt into the bowl, and process for about 5 seconds. Add the warm water to which you have added the black treacle and the oil and process for another 30 seconds by which time the mixture should look somewhat like a large mud pie, perhaps with a slightly thicker texture. If it's thoroughly blended don't process again, but take it out and place it in a large greased or non-stick loaf tin. Put it in a warm place preferably covered with a greased plastic bag and leave it to rise for about 45 minutes to 1¼ hours. It should be just coming up to the top of the tin. Put it in a hot oven, 425°F, 220°C, gas mark 7, and bake for 15 minutes, turn the heat down to 375°F, 190°C, gas mark 5, for another 30 minutes by which time the loaf should be cooked. Test it by tipping it out of the tin and tapping it on the bottom – once again it should sound hollow, if it doesn't leave it out of the tin, letting it bake for another 5 or 10 minutes until thoroughly cooked. It's best kept for a couple of days after being cooled on a wire rack or across the tin, but it can be eaten within 4 hours of being baked.

WHOLEMEAL SEED BREAD

This is one of the favourite speciality breads that I make on the basis of the standard wholemeal recipe. It is very filling and solid without being at all heavy, the perfect accompaniment to a bowl of chunky soup to turn it into a full meal. For easy slicing, leave it to cool overnight.

Attachments
double-bladed knife
plastic mixing blade

Ingredients
12 oz (350 g) wholemeal flour
1 pkt. dried ready mix yeast
7 fl oz (200 ml) warm water
½ teaspoon salt
1 tablespoon golden syrup
2 tablespoons oil
2 oz (50 g) peeled sunflower seeds
1 oz (25 g) each sesame and peeled pumpkin seeds

Method
Mix the yeast with the flour and add the warm water, salt, syrup and oil. Using the knife, process in 10 second bursts until well kneaded. This will take about 5 or 6 bursts. Decant into an oiled bowl and leave in a warm place to rise for about an hour. If you have one, replace the knife with the plastic beater, put the dough in the bowl add the seeds and process with 2 or 3 three-second bursts, just to mix in the seeds. Put in a greased medium sized bread tin to rise again, about 40 minutes. Bake at 425°F, 220°C, gas mark 7 for 45 minutes, until the bottom sounds hollow when tapped. Turn out and leave to cool thoroughly.

1 **Place the flour, yeast, warm water, salt and oil into the bowl.**

2 Add the syrup and process in 10 second bursts until well kneaded. Decant into an oiled bowl.

3 After about 1 hour return the dough to the bowl. Add the seeds and process in bursts.

4 Put the dough in a greased bread tin to rise again.

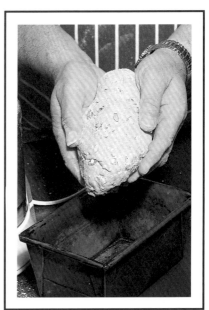

WHOLEMEAL SEED BREAD – FOR EASY SLICING LEAVE OVERNIGHT.

Soda breads really come from the late nineteenth century when artificial yeast, as baking powder used to be known, suddenly became universally available. Ireland was the great place for soda breads and indeed it still is. They don't call bread 'loaves' over there though, they call them cakes and they bake them fresh every day. None the worse for that either, as one of the great virtues of soda bread is that you can have it on the table in less than an hour, after deciding that you wanted some in the first place. It's bread to be made in the shape of giant rolls. It doesn't work too well in bread tins and one of the attractions is the lovely crust it produces.

White Soda Bread

This perhaps is the explanation of why the Irish call soda breads cakes. It has a rather cakey texture, although not at all sweet, and is really nicest eaten straight out of the oven at tea time, with a sort of high tea fry up or lots of homemade preserves and honey. Traditionally it was made with buttermilk, the slightly soured cultured produce of the dairies that Ireland is so famous for. I find it works perfectly well with a mixture of milk and water and a tablespoon of yoghurt if you happen to have it to spare.

Attachment
double-bladed knife

Ingredients
1 lb (450 g) white flour (does not have to be special bread flour for this)
2 teaspoons baking powder
1 teaspoon bicarbonate of soda
½ pint (300 ml) mixed milk and water
1 tablespoon yoghurt
½ teaspoon salt

Method
Put the flour and the salt and the baking powder in the bowl and process for 10 seconds until thoroughly mixed. Add the water, milk and yoghurt and process for 15 to 20 seconds, until the mixture forms a ball around the knife blade. Remove it, pat it firmly to make sure all the air is excluded, and shape into one or two large rolls on a greased baking sheet. Cut a large cross on the top with a sharp knife and put into a preheated oven, 400°F, 200°C, gas mark 6 without any time to allow it to rise. All the rising will take place in the oven. Bake it for 30 to 35 minutes, 20 to 25 if you are baking smaller cakes. Turn the oven down to 350°F, 180°C gas mark 4, and bake it for another 10 minutes. Make sure the cross doesn't burn, take it out and eat it while it's still warm. If you can't it can always be heated up for 5 to 10 minutes in the oven again.

Brown Soda Bread

Very similar in method to the white soda bread, this produces a very different textured loaf. It's traditionally made in Ireland, using the very soft, coarsely ground wholemeal flour to be found there. Ordinary wholemeal is fine for this side of the water and an addition is a dessertspoon of soft brown sugar, which gives the bread a little sweetness. Don't be tempted to use demerara, or any other kind of sugar, except genuine soft brown, otherwise the flavour will be lost and you'll just get a slightly sweeter loaf. I'm particularly fond of this bread at dinner parties where it can be produced almost straight from the oven, and sliced at the table, especially if the rest of the menu has got a rustic quality to it. It always produces 'Ooos' and 'Aaahs' and the only problem is you tend never to have any left, but then you can always make some the next morning so it's not too much of a hardship.

Attachment
double-bladed knife

Ingredients
1 lb (450 g) wholemeal flour (the coarser the better)
½ pint (300 ml) mixed milk and water
1 tablespoon plain yoghurt
1 dessertspoon soft brown sugar
½ teaspoon salt
2 teaspoons baking powder
1 teaspoon bicarbonate of soda

Method
Put all the dry ingredients into the bowl and process for 10 seconds. Add the milk and water mixture in which you have dissolved the sugar. Process for another 10 seconds, scrape the sides down and process again for 5 seconds until thoroughly blended. Take out the dough and if it's not quite firm enough to handle properly, add a tablespoonful or two more of flour to the mixture with the motor running. It's often difficult to determine how much liquid different wholemeals will absorb in advance. When it's at the correct texture, shape it into two loaves, on a greased baking tray, and if you've got them, cover them with either large basins or cake tins inverted over the top of them. Put them straight into a preheated oven, 425°F, 220°C, gas mark 7, and bake them for 30 minutes. Remove the tins or basins which will have helped the bread to rise quite spectacularly. Leave them to bake for another 10 minutes to set the crust and take them out of the oven. Cool them on a wire tray for about 10 to 15 minutes. You can eat them as soon as they are cool enough to cut, and if you want to reheat them in the oven the next day they still produce that lovely nutty flavour that's so characteristic of this bread.

Scones

In the west country these are normally eaten stuffed with whipped cream and strawberry jam. They are also known in America as 'biscuits', and are eaten traditionally at breakfast time.

I have given a basic recipe here to which you can add a variety of flavours and fillings, some of which I suggest at the end.

Attachment
double-bladed knife

Ingredients
8 oz (225 g) plain white flour
2 oz (50 g) butter
1 tablespoon baking powder
pinch of salt
1 teaspoon caster sugar
¼ pint (5 fl oz) milk

Method
Put all the dry ingredients into the bowl and process for 5 seconds, add the butter and process again for 5 seconds. Pour in the milk, with the motor running, until the mixture forms a ball. If it forms a ball without using all the milk, stop then; if it needs a little more milk, add it, but very gently. Take it out and roll by hand, on a slightly floured board, into a cylinder about an inch and a half across. With a sharp knife cut the cylinder into inch thick rounds and place on a greased baking tray, and pop them into a pre-heated oven 425°F, 220°C, gas mark 7. They should be ready in about 15 minutes, but if they are showing signs of browning before cooking fully inside, turn the oven down after 5 minutes to 375°F, 190°C, gas mark 5. They are really nicest eaten piping hot, straight out of the oven.

Cheese Scones

Add 4 oz (100 g) of grated cheese just before the milk, to produce the most delicious cheese scones. This is superb eaten with a little mango chutney mixed with butter spread on them.

Fruit Scones

Add an extra teaspoon of sugar, an ounce each of currants, raisins, sultanas, 4 oz (100g) of mixed dried fruit just after you've added the milk and knead in the processor for not more than 3 seconds. This makes a lovely fruit scone. I find these better not eaten hot but left to cool and mature for about 4 or 5 hours.

Herb and Onion Bread

This is a very savoury loaf, delicious enough to eat on its own and especially good with a bowl of soup. You can vary the ingredients to suit what you happen to have on the pantry shelf or growing in the garden, and you can use spring onions as opposed to the ordinary round ones I've suggested. Indeed they give a lovely green fresh flavour to the whole loaf. Do experiment with this one – a clove of garlic, a little celery leaf, all produce breads of surprisingly delicate yet rich flavour.

Attachment
double-bladed knife

Ingredients
12 oz (350 g) white bread flour
$\frac{1}{2}$ packet (1 teaspoon) instant dried yeast
8 fl oz (250 ml) water
1 tablespoon oil
1 onion
up to $\frac{1}{2}$ cup mixed green herbs – parsley, thyme, oregano and marjoram are my favourites.
If you are using dried herbs a generous teaspoon of each, with a double one of your favourite is about right
1 teaspoon salt

Method
Peel and chop the onion in the bowl and fry it very gently in the oil until translucent, but not brown. Chop the herbs, if you are using fresh ones, in the processor for 10 seconds, scrape down the sides and chop again until finely processed for about another 10 seconds. Add the flour, yeast, the onion and a teaspoon of salt and process together for 5 seconds. With the motor running add the warm water. Knead for about a minute and a quarter, making sure half way through that all the ingredients are blended in thoroughly. Put to rise in a warm draught-free place for about an hour, in a greased bowl. Process it again for just 30 seconds in the processor having knocked the air out of the dough first. Put it in a loaf tin, allow it to rise to double its volume. Bake it for 45 minutes in a preheated oven 400°F, 200°C, gas mark 6. Test to see if it is cooked by tipping it out of the tin and tapping on the base. It should sound hollow. If it's not done give it another 5 or 10 minutes. I have been known to put a layer of cheese slices along the top of this loaf about half way through cooking. After it's had a chance to rise and set properly in the oven, it makes cheese, herb and onion loaf, but that's a personal self-indulgence and I suggest you only do it the second time you try.

Crafty Cakes

I must admit that until a processor came into my life I was no cake maker. All that creaming and beating and whipping seemed to me too much like hard work, and the results never light enough or delicate enough to be worth the trouble. With my new kitchen assistant that just isn't true, and I'm almost ashamed of the amount of cakes I produce, as it's quite possible to make one a day taking about 10 minutes to do it, and to continuously astound friends, relations and family with the results. The fact is that making cakes with a processor is probably quicker than reading about how to do it. All the recipes I've given here are my family's favourites. I haven't gone in for vast complicated gâteaux, although two or three of them are quite special enough to be served as puddings in their own right after a dinner party. The chocolate gâteau, for example, is really a kind of cold soufflé, and so rich that covered with whipped cream it makes a very grand pudding indeed. By and large these are family cakes, made with fairly inexpensive and easily available ingredients, but producing the kind of results that used to be seen only in the carefully staged colour photographs of the more expensive magazines.

Chocolate cake always seems to be the favourite and these three are very different, each of them with a virtue of its own. One is from France, one from America and one from Belgium. I'll leave you to work out which is which, but do try all of them at some time or another.

CHOCOLATE OIL CAKE

Made with a very unusual set of ingredients, this cake is incredibly rich and moist, especially if kept for about a week before eating. This does not happen in my house, but if you can manage two or three days, you will find that the cake, rather than drying out, absorbs moisture from the air and becomes yummy and delicious. It's the chocolate cake I suggest you ice if you're into iced cakes, and it's marvellous made in two sections in individual flan tins, and sandwiched together with butter icing flavoured with coffee. As for the ingredients you'll just have to trust me. They may sound unusual, but they work!

Attachment
double-bladed knife

Ingredients
*6 oz (175 g) plain flour
3 heaped tablespoons cocoa
1 level teaspoon baking powder
1 level teaspoon bicarbonate of soda
5 oz (140 g) caster sugar
1 level tablespoon black treacle
2 eggs
¼ pint (5 fl oz or 150 ml) vegetable oil
¼ pint (5 fl oz or 150 ml) milk*

Method
Mix all the dry ingredients, the flour, cocoa, baking powder, bicarb and caster sugar together. Process for 10 seconds until thoroughly blended, add the liquid ingredients and process again for 30 seconds, scraping the sides of the bowl until they are all thoroughly incorporated. Pour the mixture into two greased or non-stick 7 inch (18 cm) cake tins, bake in a medium oven, 325°F, 160°C, gas mark 3 for 45 minutes. Cool and then sandwich with apricot jam, cream or butter icing as you choose.

CHOCOLATE BISCUIT CAKE

A no-cook cake made very easily, and the favourite one of all with children. I know few adults who've turned it down either! The combination of fresh orange zest with the richness of the chocolate is a classically successful combination, and as you can make it with the broken ends of biscuits left in the larder or the biscuit barrel, it can be a very economical proposition indeed.

Attachment
double-bladed knife

Ingredients
*4 oz (100 g) margarine
4 oz (100 g) drinking chocolate
1 tablespoon each golden syrup, sultanas and raisins
½ orange
8 oz (225 g) sweet biscuits (I find ginger nuts and water biscuits equally mixed the best)
2 oz (50 g) chopped nuts (optional)*

Method
Put the orange, cut into quarters, peel and all, into the bowl, process until finely chopped scraping down the sides if you need to. Add the biscuits which do not need to be in one piece, process until they are finely broken up like coarse breadcrumbs. Melt the margarine and syrup in a small saucepan and beat until smooth. Beat in the chocolate powder off the heat, add the sultanas, raisins and the chopped nuts if you're using them. Switch the motor on and pour the chocolate mixture into the processor. Process it long enough to mix it all thoroughly (about 7 seconds). Scrape it out and press into an oiled or non-stick flan tin about 8 inches (20 cm) across. It'll form a 1 inch cake which needs to be chilled in the fridge for at least 3 hours before eating.

CHOCOLATE GÂTEAU

This cake is really masquerading under a false title. It's not a cake at all but a cold chocolate soufflé. Light and rich with only just enough flour in it to help it set properly, like many chocolate cakes it's best eaten a couple of days after it's made. In this case make sure you wrap the cake when it's cool in a tea towel and put it in a tin to store. You must be careful when you're incorporating the egg whites into the mixture, because processors beat so fast they can knock the air back out of them. I myself incorporate half the egg white in the processor and fold the rest in by hand before pouring the cake into the tin to be baked.

Attachment
double-bladed knife

Ingredients
4 oz (100 g) each *self raising flour, butter, caster sugar, chocolate*
4 standard eggs

Method
Melt the butter in a saucepan adding the chocolate broken up into bits. Stir it thoroughly as it melts, not over too high a heat, so that the mixture doesn't really boil. When it's smooth, process for 5 seconds, add the sugar, process again for 15 seconds or until it's thoroughly blended. With the motor running, add the flour tablespoon by tablespoon. Separate the eggs and add the yolks to the chocolate mixture processing briefly to mix. In a separate basin whip the egg whites until they are so stiff that they stand in peaks. Add half of this to the chocolate mixture and process very briefly. Pour the chocolate mixture into the egg white basin and using a metal spoon fold in until the mixture is completely smooth. Pour it into a 7 inch (18 cm) diameter, well-greased cake tin, making sure that the tin is at least an inch and a half higher than the mixture, as it will rise spectacularly. Bake at 400°F, 200°C, gas mark 6 for 30–35 minutes. The top should be dark brown but not burnt when it's ready. Test it with a skewer which you push into the centre of the cake and which should come out clean with no mixture sticking to it. When it's cooked, put it on a rack and then wrap it in a tea towel and store it in a tin. A couple of days will improve its texture marvellously. You can eat it with a thick layer of icing sugar on the top, smothered in double cream, or just as it is for a delicious, slightly gooey chocolate cake.

Streusel Cake

This is a cake with a crumble topping. The crunchy topping and the soft rich cake make a lovely contrast. It's the sort of confection they serve with coffee in the famous cafés of Vienna and Salzburg, but it's quite good, I find, at coffee time in Walton-on-Thames or Selkirk. Either way, the secret, as usual, is the processor which makes very light work of the two separate processes of rubbing in that have to be done to get the combination of textures.

Attachment
double-bladed knife

Ingredients
6 oz (175 g) plain flour
2 oz (50 g) cornflour
2 teaspoons baking powder
4 oz (100 g) butter or soft margarine
4 oz (100 g) caster sugar
2 eggs
6 tablespoons milk

For the topping
1½ oz (40 g) plain flour
2 oz (50 g) demerara sugar
1½ oz (40 g) butter
1 tablespoon cinnamon

Method
Begin by making the topping. Place the flour, sugar, cinnamon and butter in the bowl and process until it resembles very fine dry crumbs. Take it out and keep aside, then put all the cake ingredients – the flour, cornflour, baking powder, butter, sugar, eggs and milk into the bowl, and process for 15 seconds, scrape down the sides, process again for another 10 seconds. Turn it into a buttered 7 inch (18 cm) cake tin or one of those Viennese-style tins with a hole in the middle. Sprinkle the crumble mixture on the top and bake at 375°C, 190°C, gas mark 5 for about an hour. When it's cooked turn it out carefully, being sure not to spill all the topping. You can eat this cake while it's still just a little warm which, when you consider the smells which it gives out when baking, is a great relief to the test of self-control.

FOR PHOTOGRAPH TURN TO PAGE 113.

Marmalade Cake

Another cake that's particularly useful for using up odds and ends. If you've got a couple of odd jars with bits of marmalade in the bottom and you can manage to get together three round tablespoons, you've got the basic ingredients for this cake. It's got a marvellous delicate flavour, and although it can be cooked in any container you like, it's best cooked in a loaf tin and sliced across into slices like bread. No butter needed with this one for it tastes quite rich enough without any help, thank you. As with most processor cakes, put all the ingredients in at the same time which keeps it light and avoids over-beating.

Attachment
double-bladed knife

Ingredients
8 oz (225 g) plain flour
1 teaspoon baking powder
4 oz (100 g) soft margarine or butter
3½ oz (90 g) sugar
2 eggs
3 large tablespoons orange marmalade (or a mixture of other marmalades and jams)
grated rind of a large orange
grated rind of a small lemon

Method
Put all the ingredients into the bowl and process for 15–20 seconds. You may have bits of marmalade rind still left in the mixture, but don't let that worry you, as it will make delicious little nibbly bits. Tip the whole mixture into a large loaf tin, spread the top smooth, spinkle with just a teaspoon or so of caster sugar, bake at 375°F, 190°C, gas mark 5 for three quarters of an hour to an hour. You may need to bake it a little longer if the tin is particularly narrow and deep. Test it by running a skewer into it – it should come out absolutely clean. Cool on a wire rack.

OPPOSITE: MARMALADE CAKE (LEFT) HAS A MARVELLOUS DELICATE FLAVOUR IN CONTRAST TO THE RICH AND DELICIOUS GOLDEN FRUIT CAKE (RIGHT)

BANANA TEABUN

Although you can eat this with butter, it's not really a bun at all, but a kind of rich, fruity, loaf-shaped cake. It's also the perfect way for using up bananas that have gone over the hill a bit and are squashed, for even if the skins are completely black, they're still OK for this recipe.

Attachment
double-bladed knife

Ingredients
8 oz (225 g) self raising flour
½ teaspoon salt
4 oz (100 g) butter – softened
6 oz (175 g) caster sugar
6 oz (175 g) mixed dried fruit
2 eggs
1 lb (450 g) bananas

Method
Put all the ingredients except the dried fruit into the bowl and process until they are all thoroughly amalgamated and the bananas chopped up fine; the odd chunk doesn't matter, but they shouldn't be in large pieces. Add the dried fruit and process for just 3 or 4 seconds to mix the fruit in, but not to chop it. Pour the mixture into a buttered or non-stick 2 lb (900 g) loaf tin, spread it out evenly and bake it at 350°F, 180°C, gas mark 4 for an hour and a half. Let it cool before you tip it out of the tin. It will keep for two or three days, with no harm at all, before you eat it.

GOLDEN FRUIT CAKE

This recipe really is, I'm afraid, a cause for shame. It's like one of those cakes that people used to spend hours in the making but with a processor it cannot be stretched out, once you've got the ingredients together, to more than a minute and a half, except of course for the baking time. The only thing to do is to pretend you don't have a processor, and spent two hours making the cake. No one ever believes anything different anyway, because it just tastes too good. It's also the basis for an even richer dark fruit cake for Christmas and birthday type celebrations, and I suggest at the end of the recipe a way of amending it to include that. The basic recipe though is pretty rich and delicious in its own right.

Attachment
double-bladed knife

Ingredients
6 oz (175 g) self raising flour
3 oz (75 g) soft brown sugar
3 oz (75 g) butter (softened) or soft margarine
1½ tablespoons milk
2 medium eggs
1 teaspoon mixed spice
3 oz (75 g) each, raisins, sultanas and mixed peel
1 oz (25 g) flaked almonds

Method
Put the flour, eggs, butter, sugar and milk into the mixing bowl. Process for about 15 seconds, scrape down the sides of the bowl and process again for 10 seconds making sure that the whole mixture is thoroughly blended. Add the fruit, nuts and spice, process for just 5 seconds to blend them in, but not chopped up. Pour the whole mixture into an 8 inch (20 cm) greased cake tin (or a non-stick one), and cook in a slow oven, 325°F, 160°C, gas mark 3 for two hours before testing by running a skewer into the centre. It may need up to an extra half an hour's cooking. If the top starts to brown before the centre is finished, cover it with a little foil just to keep it from going too crisp. Cool it on a wire rack for at least two or three hours, and then either store it or ice it in any way you please.

FOR PHOTOGRAPH TURN TO PAGE 117 (TOP).

CELEBRATION FRUIT CAKE

To the previous recipe add, at the same time as the fruit, a tablespoonful of dark treacle, the grated juice and rind of a lemon and 2 oz (50 g) of glacé cherries. Bake as above. Some people find that washing the sugary bits off the outside of the cherries and then drying them helps to stop them sinking in the cake. Personally, I find that they sink or not as the wind takes them, and no amount of washing will stop it. Either way, they taste delicious and are worth it even in a delicate pink layer across the bottom of each slice.

STRAWBERRY SHORTCAKE

Although strawberries are available all the year round these days, this cake I think is still best served in the wonderful period in June and July when English strawberries, juicier and sweeter at their best than anything from abroad, are with us. It is originally an American cake, though why it should have been left to them to invent this wonderful way of serving strawberries I don't know. I feel we do undervalue strawberries – perhaps this recipe will help to remedy that.

Attachment
double-bladed knife

Ingredients
6 oz (175 g) butter
3 oz (75 g) caster sugar
10 oz (300 g) self raising flour
pinch of salt

Filling
8 oz (225 g) strawberries
a small carton of double cream or fromage frais

Method
Put the butter and sugar into the processor and cream until smooth and pale and fluffy, add the flour and the salt and mix those in, in short 5 second bursts. Put the mixture into an 8 inch tin, smooth it until it is level and prick the surface, bake it 350°F, 180°C, gas mark 4 for 20–23 minutes. It should be golden but not brown. When cool, split it horizontally with a sharp knife. Put in half the cream or fromage frais which you have whipped until it is light, top with split strawberries then the remaining half of the cake. Top with the other half of the cream and decorate with one or two strawberries you have reserved specially for the purpose. It can sit in the fridge for a couple of hours but don't chill it for too long because the cream and strawberries will start to deteriorate after that time.

VICTORIA SPONGE

Until the little helper came into my kitchen sponges were always a mystery to me and came out like crunchy pancakes. Now crafty sponges flavoured with orange, lemon or even chocolate are a matter quite literally of three minutes plus the time they take to cook. My reputation is transformed and my waistline totally destroyed. However, if you have a family that's used to practising self-denial or you don't really mind what happens to your shape, try making one or two variations of these special teatime treats.

Attachment
double-bladed knife

Ingredients
6 oz (175 g) soft butter or soft margarine
6 oz (175 g) sugar
3 eggs
6 oz (175 g) self raising flour

Method
Put all the ingredients into the mixing bowl and process for 10–15 seconds, scrape down the sides and process for another 10 or 15. Don't process it too long or the cake will become overbeaten and dry. Grease two sponge tins (or use non-stick), spread the mixture into them using the spatula to make sure it's even across the top, and bake at 350°F, 180°C, gas mark 4 for about 25 minutes. Don't keep opening and shutting the door but near the end of the cooking time you can test the sponge by pressing it in the centre; if your fingermark vanishes and the sponge rises up again, it's cooked. Turn them onto a wire rack to let them cool. My favourite method is to use one of those extremely expensive, delicious strawberry jams and spread it thickly in the middle before dusting the top with icing sugar, but you can follow your own inclinations. I'm afraid that's all there is to it. It really is as simple as it sounds and with a processor there's no way you can make it more difficult.

1&2 **Put all the ingredients into the bowl and process for 10 or 15 seconds. Scrape down the sides and process for another 10 or 15 seconds.**

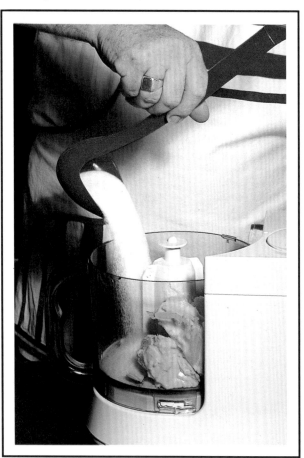

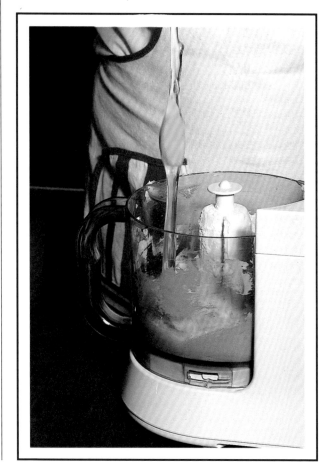

LEMON SPONGE

Grate the rind of half a lemon and cut the remaining half of lemon, peel and all into quarters. Before you put anything else into the bowl process the grated lemon rind and the half lemon for 20 seconds until you have a fine smooth mixture. Proceed as above, adding the flour, fat, sugar and eggs and bake, also as above. Lemon icing is nicest on top, with a thick layer of lemon marmalade in the middle. The jelly

kind is fine, but if you can find some with peel it's even more delicious.

CHOCOLATE SPONGE

Dissolve three level tablespoons of cocoa in three tablespoons of hot water and add to the other ingredients before processing. When iced this makes a perfect cake for birthdays and celebrations.

3 **Using a spatula, spread the mixture into two greased or non-stick sponge tins.**

4 **Don't keep opening and shutting the oven door – test near the end of the cooking time.**

VICTORIA SPONGE – A SPECIAL TEATIME TREAT.

COFFEE AND HAZELNUT CAKE

This is another cake which is made with oil rather than butter, like the chocolate oil cake on page 114. These cakes are easy to make in the processor, taking very little time indeed and have the added advantage of being particularly low in saturated fat. This one is delicious and has a super nutty flavour to complement the coffee which is the underlying theme of the gâteau. You can serve it as it comes or split it and fill it with a butter cream made from 2 oz (50 g) butter and 4 oz (100 g) icing sugar with a teaspoon of instant coffee dissolved in a tablespoon of water, all mixed together in a processor until they are thoroughly blended.

Attachment
double-bladed knife

Ingredients
3 oz (75 g) hazelnuts or hazelnut pieces
3 oz (75 g) caster sugar
4 oz (100 g) self raising flour
3 eggs
2 teaspoons instant coffee
2 tablespoons soya oil
1 teaspoon baking powder

Method
Put the hazelnuts into the processor and grind to a fairly fine powder, add all the other ingredients, the sugar, flour, eggs, the instant coffee which you have dissolved in 2 tablespoons of water, the oil and the baking powder and process thoroughly, in 2 bursts of 5 seconds scraping the bowl down between them. Grease and flour a 7 inch (18 cm) sandwich tin and pour in the mixture, smoothing the top down. Pre-heat the oven to 350°F, 180°C, gas mark 4 and bake for approximately 25 minutes, until the cake is brown and has shrunk away from the sides of the tin a little. Turn onto a rack, and when cool you can split in two and sandwich together with either a little apricot jam, or with the butter cream filling explained above. Decorate with a few split hazelnuts if you have any to spare.

Proven Puddings

These, as the song says, are some of my favourite things. I'm a great believer, like the French, in finishing a meal with a sweet taste in the mouth rather than the tang of cheese. I'm not a believer, however, in a great deal of hard work going into making a pudding; by the time the rest of the meal is ready the cook needs a bit of rest and relaxation too. This is a collection of puds, all of which can be made without a processor, but using a processor is easier and quicker, so you won't finish up with a bunch of grapes to go with the cheese or a bought-in cake. These puds range from the grand, a very sophisticated Almond Mousse, through the rustic Clafoutis, to the extremely simple – the recipe for real custard which you really must try even if it's only to pour over an apple pie.

Now we are all much more aware of the importance of lowering the amount of fat in our diet it is worth mentioning that in all these recipes where cream, particularly double cream, is mentioned, there are alternative ways that reduce the fat content quite dramatically. A safe bet whenever you are using double cream to whip, for example, is to use half the volume of double cream and half the volume of plain yoghurt, whip the cream in the normal way and then add the yoghurt spoonful by spoonful; it will stand up almost as firm as pure cream, contain only half the fat and taste delicious. Very reminiscent of the French crème fraiche that is so central to modern French-style cooking.

With these creams, custards and fruit fools, presentation is crucial and I'm very fond of using elegant and unusual wine glasses, white china or tiny little soufflé dishes made from very pale French porcelain. Try and avoid fussy patterned crockery for these puddings, for the pale fruit colours look much better against simple backgrounds.

Why fruit fools are called fools is something I've never actually been able to discover. What they are is a very traditional mixture of fruit and cream or custard, blended together to make a particularly enticing and really rather rich dish. You don't need a lot of these. The flavour's very intense, and they're very filling.

BOODLES FOOL

Boodles was and still is one of the clubs for gentlemen in St James's in London, famous for its food, but no one who's an outsider gets in to sample it. The odd recipe has escaped and this is one of them. It's very simple to make, and is said to date back to the seventeenth century. Serve it if you can in clear wine glasses with enough room for a good layer of the cake crumbs at the bottom before you pour on the orange cream.

Attachment
double-bladed knife

Ingredients
8 oz (225 g) sponge cake (dry is fine, but make sure it isn't too stale)
1/2 pint (300 ml) whipping cream or 1/4 pint (150 ml) double cream and 1/4 pint plain yoghurt
1/4 pint (150 ml) orange juice (carton is OK, tinned is not)
1/2 a whole orange

Method
Put the sponge cake into the mixing bowl, and process to fine breadcrumbs. Tip out and mix with half the orange juice. Whip the cream, adding the remaining orange juice as you go, until the cream is beaten thick and all the juice is incorporated. Put the half orange into the bowl and process until it's finely puréed, and beat that into the cream as well. Put a portion of the crumbs into the bottom of each glass and pour over some of the cream. You can use a slice of orange from the other half to decorate each top. It's much the best if it's left to set in the refrigerator for about half an hour before it's served.

GOOSEBERRY FOOL

This is perhaps the most traditional of all English puddings, apple tart and jam roly-poly not withstanding. It's very simple and very cheap, and ideally is made with custard (see page 126) as it used to be in the Middle Ages rather than with cream. Cream is fine, but it produces a rather more delicate and sharp pudding. This is particularly nice served with very thin, crisp ginger biscuits.

Attachment
double-bladed knife

Ingredients
1 lb (450 g) fresh gooseberries (a tin will do, but it really isn't the same)
6 oz (175 g) sugar
1/2 pint (300 ml) whipping cream or 1/2 pint custard (it must be real) or 1/4 pint (150 ml) double cream and 1/4 pint natural yoghurt

Method
Top and tail the gooseberries and wash them, putting them without any extra water into a pan. Add the sugar and simmer gently, the juice running out of the gooseberries will provide all the liquid you need. When they're cooked and squashy – about 15 minutes – pour the whole lot into the food processor. Switch on and process for 10 seconds, scrape down the sides and process again. The fruit should be thoroughly puréed although it may have a little texture left in it at the end if you like. If you're using cream, whip it until it's thick but not stiff and pour it into the bowl, switch on and process for 5 seconds. If you're using custard, let it get cold before adding it and process again in the bowl. This time you may need to process for a little longer, about 10 seconds is right. Pour the gooseberry fool either into china soufflé dishes or into wine glasses if you prefer. Let it set in the fridge for at least an hour. This is a sharp, clean-tasting dish, so reminiscent of spring-time in Britain.

You can substitute a whole range of fruit for the gooseberries – strawberries, blackcurrants and apricots are my favourites. The process is exactly the same, but you may want a little less sugar with fruit sweeter than gooseberries.

FOR PHOTOGRAPH TURN TO PAGE 123.

REAL CUSTARD

Believe it or not, custard didn't always come out of packets, and wasn't always that bright comic-strip yellow. Real custard is amazingly simple to make, extremely delicious to eat and, funnily enough, it doesn't take much longer than the packet stuff. You can use it for many different purposes, eat it on its own, as a basis for fruit fools, replacing double cream (a much cheaper way of making a fool and even less foolish!) or you can use it in the traditional way over a variety of tarts, pies or puddings.

Attachment
double-bladed knife

Ingredients
½ pint (300 ml) milk
1 tablespoon cornflour
1 egg
1 egg yolk
2 tablespoons caster sugar
1 teaspoon vanilla essence

Method
Put the egg, egg yolk and vanilla essence into the bowl, switch on, and with the motor running, add the cornflour followed by the sugar. Bring the milk to the boil and just as it comes up, pour it in through the feed-tube, again with the motor running. Switch off after 3 or 4 seconds, when the mixture is thoroughly blended. Put it back into the saucepan and over a very low heat (you can use a double boiler for this) heat it gently. It'll thicken in about one minute and be cooked in about two. It can be eaten hot or cold, and is equally delicious either way.

CLAFOUTIS

A fantastic thick, crunchy pancake made traditionally in south west France with the bitter cherries that grow there and which have a short but splendid season. Unfortunately, we rarely get those cherries over here, but this dish can be made with the black cherries that we do get or with apples mixed with cinnamon. It's particularly nice as a culmination to a family lunch or a big dinner party among friends when the food's had a strong rustic quality. It's not delicate, and it's pretty filling, so make sure the people who are going to eat it are hungry. Nor is it a dish to keep waiting once it's cooked, as it is really at its best when it comes piping hot out of the oven.

The secret of a good clafoutis is the beating of the sugar and flour into the batter mixture so that it's really totally incorporated. A process which can take time, except for your friendly processor and the crafty clafoutis method.

Attachment
double-bladed knife

Ingredients
5 eggs
5 oz (150 g) each *icing sugar and plain flour*
1 lb (450 g) cherries (ideally stoned) or
1 lb (450 g) cooking apples, cored and peeled
2 oz (50 g) sugar with 1 teaspoon cinnamon mixed in
1 tablespoon oil

Method
Break the eggs into the bowl, turn on and with the motor running add the icing sugar and flour tablespoon by tablespoon, one of each alternately, through the feed-tube. The end should be a smooth batter. As soon as all the flour and sugar are used, add one tablespoon of oil and switch off. Butter a large baking dish or one of those crinkly-sided white china pie dishes. Pour in the batter mixture and sprinkle over it the cherries or the chopped up apple, cinnamon and sugar mixture. If you're using just the cherries, a little caster sugar sprinkled over the top will provide a nice caramelised grainy coating. Bake it at 350°F, 180°C, gas mark 4 for approximately an hour. It should be risen and golden to the touch, but the fruit should be buried in the crispy thick pancake.

1 **Place the eggs in the bowl. Process whilst adding alternate tablespoons of icing sugar and flour.**

2 Add the oil immediately after the flour and sugar. Pour into a dish.

3 Sprinkle over the cherries followed by the caster sugar or chopped apple, cinnamon and sugar mixture.

CLAFOUTIS – A TRADITIONAL RECIPE FROM SOUTH WEST FRANCE.

CHOCOLATE MOUSSE

One of the dishes that has become debased in the course of time because everybody serves it and every restaurant has one, but very few people have ever tasted a perfectly made chocolate mousse. One of the reasons for this is that in order to make one, an enormous amount of hard beating by hand has to take place, or at least it used to until processors appeared in the kitchen. Do not skimp on the butter. It makes a great difference to the way this version of chocolate mousse tastes.

Attachment
double-bladed knife

Ingredients
7 oz (200 g) bitter chocolate (Bourneville's OK; Suchard or Terry's bitter chocolate is even better, there's less sugar in it)
3 oz (75 g) unsalted butter
6 eggs, separated
juice and grated rind of an orange

Method
Put the juice of the orange into a small heavy saucepan. Break the chocolate up into small squares, and add it to the juice and melt over a very low heat stirring all the time. When the chocolate has completely melted, add the butter and stir it in. When both are properly melted, pour the mixture into the bowl, switch on and process three times, 10 seconds each, scraping down the sides in between. This beating is very important and must go on until the whole chocolate mixture is smooth and glistening in texture. With the motor running add the egg yolks one at a time through the feed-tube, and process for a further 10 seconds before pouring the mixture back into the saucepan and stirring it over the very lowest heat for just 1 minute. (Do not let it boil or the eggs will scramble.) Whip the egg whites in a separate basin until they are so stiff you can turn the basin upside down and then gently fold the chocolate mixture into the egg whites, turning it all until it's all firmly mixed together. Add the grated rind from the orange, and pour into one large or six individual bowls and chill in the fridge for a least 3 hours.

HOMEMADE ICE CREAM

Ice cream made at home is one of cooking's great revelations. Homemade bread and homemade soup join it as being one of the set of three things that are always better made at home. Part of the reason for this is the quality of ingredients that you use, and although it may sound extravagant at first, you will find that because of its smoothness and richness a portion of ice cream goes a very long way. I've given a basic vanilla ice cream recipe, and three flavour variations, which I'm sure will all become fast favourites with your family. Your guests will enjoy them too, if your family will let them get to any.

Attachment
double-bladed knife

Ingredients
3 eggs
4 oz (100 g) icing sugar
1 teaspoon vanilla essence
5 oz (150 g) whipping cream

Method
Break the eggs into the bowl (for an even richer ice cream use up to 6 egg yolks replacing each egg with 2 yolks) add the vanilla essence, turn the motor on and feed the icing sugar in, tablespoon by tablespoon. Process until the mixture is a pale creamy yellow and very much thickened. In a separate bowl whip the cream until it is thick but not stiff. Add the egg and sugar mixture to the cream and stir until thoroughly amalgamated. Pour it into a deep plastic bowl or container and put it into your freezer, if you've got one, or the freezing part of your fridge with the fridge turned up to maximum. It needs to freeze for at least 4 hours and afterwards will benefit from half an hour in the ordinary part of the fridge just before serving. If it sounds almost too simple – it is!

FRUIT ICE CREAM

You can add to this ice cream in a number of different ways. My favourites are fruit purées and the crunchy almond brittle known as praline. I'm going to give the recipe for strawberry ice cream but you can substitute peaches, apricots, raspberries or blackcurrants as long as the purée is thick and creamy like pouring double cream. You may need to thicken one or two of the more watery fruits with a teaspoon of cornflour while cooking.

Add to one recipe of ice cream 8 oz (225 g) strawberries (which do not need to be in the prime of life), hull them, wash them and cook them with a tablespoon of sugar for 3 to 4 minutes until the juice is just starting to run, process them to a purée and add them to the mixture of eggs and sugar before you mix it all into the cream. After that, proceed exactly the same way, chilling the mixture as before.

A crafty flavouring for when fresh fruit is unavailable is marmalade – use about 4 tablespoons to one recipe of ice cream. Add to the sugar and egg mixture, process until the marmalade is incorporated, then proceed as above.

Frozen yoghurt is set to be the pudding of the 1990s – it swept America and is catching on in Britain. There is nothing quite as easy to make as frozen yoghurt at home if you have got an ice cream maker to help you, as the machines have a paddle that beats mixture as it freezes thus getting rid of the icicles left by a processor. However, you can manage quite well without by beating the mixture half way through the freezing process and getting rid of the icicles that way. I have suggested a basic recipe again here, with a number of variations in flavouring which I find particularly delicious.

BASIC YOGHURT ICE CREAM

Attachment
double-bladed knife

Ingredients
1 pint (½ litre) of plain (preferably whole milk) yoghurt
2 tablespoons honey
1 teaspoon vanilla essence
1 dessertspoon cornflour
6 fl oz (1 breakfast cup) of milk
3 oz (75 g) caster sugar

Method
Put the caster sugar, cornflour and milk into the processor bowl and process until well mixed, pour into a saucepan, preferably non-stick and heat through until thickened. Put the yoghurt, honey, milk and cornflour mixture, which you have allowed to cool a little, back into the processor and blend thoroughly. If you have an ice cream maker, pour into this and switch on; if not, put it into a plastic tub (the kind in which ice cream comes from the shops) and freeze in the coldest part of your freezer for 2 hours. Take out, scrape the mixture out of the tub, put it back into the processor, whisk until smooth, about 10–15 seconds is right, pour it back in the tub and freeze again for 2 hours before eating.

GINGER AND HONEY FROZEN YOGHURT

Substitute 2 more tablespoons of honey for the caster sugar and add 2 tablespoons of ginger in syrup to the yoghurt on the final processing before freezing. Process until the ginger is finely chopped but not completely puréed.

RASPBERRY FROZEN YOGHURT

Proceed as in the basic recipe but substitute for the honey 4 oz (100 g) raspberries which you have cooked with 2 oz (50 g) of sugar for 5 minutes over a gentle heat until they have just softened. Add these at the same time as you add the cornflour mixture and process lightly before freezing.

GREEN TEA FROZEN YOGHURT

An unusual suggestion this, but absolutely delicious and very refreshing. You use gunpowder or Japanese green tea, available in most speciality shops and some supermarkets. Don't be tempted to use Jasmine tea as it has not got the right flavour balance. Make the frozen yoghurt as you would in the basic recipe substituting the tea which you have brewed to a strong consistency (3 teaspoons of tea to 1 pint (about ½ litre) of water) instead of the milk when making the mixture with cornflour.

PRALINE ICE CREAM

This is a very high-grade ice cream, the kind served in very delicate, very expensive cups in expensive restaurants.

Attachment
double-bladed knife

Ingredients
knob of butter
4 oz (100 g) whole, unblanched almonds
4 tablespoons caster sugar
basic ice cream ingredients

Method
Put a knob of butter into a thick saucepan, preferably non-stick, and add the almonds and toss them until coated with the butter and browned even more on the outside. Add the sugar and stir into the almonds until it is thoroughly melted and the whole lot is beginning to pop. Be careful at this stage because if it pops onto you it can burn quite nastily. As soon as the sugar has caramelised and is starting to turn golden brown and toffee-coloured, switch the heat off and leave the pan on one side. After 2 or 3 minutes immerse just the base of it in cold water. This will have the effect of contracting the pan suddenly and shaking the praline loose (that's why a non-stick pan is particularly advantageous at this stage). Tip it out onto a sheet of greaseproof paper and let it cool completely. When the praline is cool, break it into 1 inch chunks and process until it's really quite a fine powder. It'll make a noise doing this, but don't let it worry you, the machine can handle it quite easily. To make ice cream, add the powder to the cream, not the egg mixture, before you fold it all in together. When you freeze it you can decorate it if you like with one or two of the larger chunks of praline that you may have kept aside.

Low Fat Christmas Pudding

This is one of my great triumphs. Not only is the dish delicious but it is also almost unbearably good for you. Instead of the normal high fat 50 per cent suet Christmas pudding that is normally served, this one has no fat in it at all.

Attachment
double-bladed knife

Ingredients (for 8)
1 lb (450 g) brown breadcrumbs (see method)
4 oz (100 g) brazil nuts
1 oz (25 g) almonds
8 oz (225 g) grated apple
8 oz (225 g) sultanas
8 oz (225 g) currants
8 oz (225 g) dates
8 oz (225 g) demerara sugar
4 oz (100 g) mixed peel
2 bananas
rind and juice of a lemon
1 teaspoon salt
2 teaspoons mixed spice
3 eggs
½ pint (300 ml) milk

Method
Cut the crusts off 4 thick slices of wholemeal bread, cut into quarters and process until fine breadcrumbs. Add the brazil nuts and almonds, grated apple, the dates, the lemon rind and the bananas. Process in 5 second bursts until well chopped and mixed. Add the sultanas and currants, demerara sugar, the mixed peel, the juice of the lemon, the salt, the mixed spice, the eggs and the milk and process briefly again in 1 or 2 second bursts so as not to chop up the soft fruit but to mix the mixture together. Put it into two 2-pint (1 litre), or if you are feeling very grand, one 4-pint (2 litre) pudding basin, cover with greaseproof paper and then a pleated cover of foil tied down. Boil it for 3 hours (or 1 hour in a pressure cooker) and then just before eating, heat for another 45 minutes to 1 hour (or 30 minutes in the pressure cooker). Serve it as usual flamed with rum and with cream or hard sauce. Don't keep this pudding except under refrigeration for more than 2 months as it doesn't have very high storage qualities.

Steamed Ginger Pudding

I am particularly fond of ginger; in fact I have a passion for it in all forms whether Chinese preserves, ginger beer, sautéed with strips of beef in a stir-fry or in a steamed pudding like this one. This is an 18th-century style pudding brought up to date by making it in the processor.

Attachment
double-bladed knife

Ingredients
4 oz (100 g) self raising flour
3 oz (75 g) softened butter
3 oz (75 g) sugar
2 eggs
3 oz (75 g) preserved ginger in syrup
1 teaspoon ground ginger (or a dessertspoon ground ginger and 2 tablespoons golden syrup)
2 tablespoons milk

Method
Put the preserved ginger, if using it, and its syrup into the processor and process until finely chopped. Add the butter, sugar, flour, eggs, ginger powder and milk and process until well blended. Butter a pudding basin which will take it comfortably – it should be at least 2 pints (1 litre) – and pour in the mixture. Cover with greaseproof paper, tie round with string and steam for 2 hours in a conventional steamer or 45 minutes to 1 hour in a pressure cooker. This is particularly delicious served hot with real egg custard (page 126).

Simple Shakes

I have included a few milk shakes, both conventional and unconventional, to provide special treats for you and your family. While it's really not a standard blender the processor can work perfectly well in this particular rôle and can manage to handle materials that an ordinary blender would blanch at. I've given a few recipes for children's-type milk shakes here, chocolate and strawberry, and a banana, lemon and honey flavoured one which I think they will really enjoy. There are also one or two grown-up milk shakes as well as the famous breakfast-in-a-glass recipe that swept America recently and has been craftily adapted for our own use over here.

Avocado And Pineapple

A milk shake with a slightly sophisticated 'grown-up' flavour which I'm sure will appeal to the kids. It is nice either as a first course at a summer dinner party or as a milk shake in its own right.

Attachment
double-bladed knife

Ingredients
1 very ripe avocado
1 small tin pineapple chunks in syrup
5 oz (150 g) carton yoghurt
¹/₂ pint (300 ml) ice cold milk
sprigs of mint
pinch salt

Method
Cut the avocado in half, remove the stone, and spoon the flesh into the bowl. Add the pineapple and the syrup from the tin, a pinch of salt (trust me) and the yoghurt and process for 15 seconds. Scrape down the sides and process again until smooth. Add the milk and process until the whole mixture is frothy. You can add a few of the mint leaves at this stage and process again for 2 seconds to mix them in, or you can leave them as sprigs to decorate the milk shake when you pour it into tall glasses. Chill in the fridge for 30 minutes before serving.
FOR PHOTOGRAPH TURN TO PAGE 131.

Chocolate Milk Shake

Straight out of the McDonalds stable but much cheaper to make at home than to buy. You may need one of those enormously thick straws to drink it with, an ordinary straw just hasn't got a chance with the thickness of this particular shake.

Attachment
double-bladed knife

Ingredients
8 oz (225 g) chocolate ice cream
¹/₂ pint (300 ml) ice cold milk
bar chocolate flake

Method
Put the milk into the bowl, add half the ice cream and switch on, then add the rest of the ice cream through the feed-tube, spoonful by spoonful, until the shake is thoroughly blended. Don't process it for more than 25 seconds otherwise it may start to warm up a bit. Crumble the flake in your hand and add it through the feed-tube to the shake, saving enough to decorate the top. Pour it into tall glasses and sprinkle over the remaining flake bits. Put in the thick straws and duck, as the kids come rushing to you.

Banana, Lemon And Honey

A simple, very nutritious shake which adults and children both seem to like. You can use old and fairly tired bananas for this recipe on condition that they're properly ripe.

Attachment
double-bladed knife

Ingredients
4 bananas
juice of a lemon
2 tablespoons runny honey
5 oz (150 g) yoghurt
5 fl oz (150 ml) milk

Method
Peel the bananas and cut them into 1 inch slices, put them in the processor with the lemon juice and the honey. Start the motor and with it running add the yoghurt, then fill the yoghurt pot again with milk and add that. You'll get a golden coloured, very thick shake. If you like your shakes a little thinner add an extra measure of milk. Chill and serve in tall glasses, perhaps with a banana slice or two on the top.

Strawberry Milk Shake

Another standard favourite, but with the added bonus of fresh strawberries incorporated in it. You can use the strawberries raw or cooked as you please. I find that adults prefer the rather sharper taste of the raw strawberries, and kids the cooked version. Either way, the ingredients are the same.

Attachment
double-bladed knife

Ingredients
8 oz (225 g) strawberries hulled and washed
2 tablespoons caster sugar
4 oz (100 g) vanilla ice cream – not strawberry (dairy grade is best)
1/2 pint (300 ml) cold milk

Method
Save two or three of the prettier strawberries for decoration and, if you want the children's version, cook the strawberries and sugar together for 2 or 3 minutes until the juice is running. If you want the strawberries raw, put the strawberries and sugar straight into the bowl. Either way, purée the fruit and sugar mixture, add the ice cream and the cold milk all at once and process again until smooth. Decorate with the whole fresh strawberries, and chill in the fridge for 10 minutes or so before consuming. It's sometimes so thick that you have to finish it off with a spoon. I find this no hardship.

BREAKFAST IN A GLASS

An American habit, and not as nauseating as it sounds, is a drinking breakfast. Too many people skip breakfast these days, because of pressure, time and lack of desire to eat a whole lot of greasy food early in the morning. This recipe gives you a light and delicious breakfast, which you really can drink from the glass. It's made in a trice and is full of good things as well as nice flavours. I find it's particularly good as part of a weekend brunch when of course it isn't the whole of your breakfast but merely the start.

Attachment
double-bladed knife

Ingredients
1 whole orange
5 oz (150 g) plain yoghurt
2 teaspoons honey
1 egg
½ pint (300 ml) cold milk
2 dessertspoons wheatgerm

Method
Cut the orange into quarters, take out any pips, cut each quarter in half and put them into the bowl. Add the egg and yoghurt, and process until the orange is finely blended (believe it or not, the peel won't taste bitter). With the motor running, add the milk and then 2 tablespoons of runny honey. Blend again until smoothly mixed, pour into two glasses, and sprinkle the wheatgerm over the top. You can eat it with a spoon, or drink it. It's a slower process drinking than eating, but equally delicious either way. It can be made the night before and left in the fridge covered with a piece of cling-film, but add the wheatgerm at the last minute.

Vegetarian Alternatives

Over recent years vegetarianism has ceased to become a cranky, beards and sandals and dirndl skirts affair and has become very central to eating in Britain. It is estimated that there are something like 2 to 2½ million full time vegetarians and an enormously large number of people, it may be up to 10 million, who are halfway there; who eat some fish, maybe a little white meat, chicken and turkey but don't touch red meat any more. Not only has it become fashionable and acceptable, it is also now realised that this particular sort of eating can also be extremely healthy and good for you. While I am not a vegetarian, a couple of members of my family are pretty close and I have great sympathy with the approach. What I don't

have great sympathy with though is the lack of imagination that is sometimes applied to vegetarian food. I know plenty of homes and restaurants where vegetarians just get the vegetables to eat without the meat, or they get the inevitable omelette or quiche as their main course. There is nothing wrong with either of those but it is possible to cook really interesting main course meals without meat, or fish come to that! Here are five of my favourites from the simple to the grand, the grand being the sort of dish that you serve at Christmas for your vegetarian family member. You may then find that the carnivores amongst you are eating it as much as the vegetarians because it tastes so delicious.

STUFFED AUBERGINES

Aubergines are known in the Middle East as the poor man's caviare and they are a very solid filling vegetable with a very chewy and substantial texture. This is really an adaptation (as is the vegetarian moussaka on page 137) of a Middle Eastern dish, called in Turkey *Imam Bayeldi*, which literally means the Imam, or spiritual teacher, fainted. Some think he fainted because of the incredibly delicious flavour and others believe it was the thought of the cost of something that tasted so good. You can serve it hot as a main course with rice pilau, or cold in smaller portions as a starter.

Attachments
slicing disc
double-bladed knife

Ingredients
2 large aubergines
1 large or 2 medium sized onions
1 clove garlic
8 oz (225 g) ripe tomatoes
6 tablespoons tomato passata (thick tomato sauce that comes in tetrapacks)
4 oz (100 g) olive oil
2 oz (50 g) pine nuts
2 tablespoons chopped parsley
salt

Method
Peel and quarter the onion and peel and trim the garlic, put them into the processor with the tomatoes de-stalked and quartered and process until a fairly smooth mixture. Heat half the olive oil in a saucepan, add the mixture and turn in the oil for 2 minutes, add the tomato purée and a little water if it seems dry and cook very gently making sure it doesn't dry out for 20 minutes. Meanwhile, cut the aubergines in half lengthways, score into the cut side with a knife, put a teaspoon of salt on each side and leave them to drain in a colander for 20 minutes. This gets out the bitter juice that is in some aubergines; rinse them thoroughly to get rid of the salt, put them on a baking tray and spoon over and into the slits in each aubergine a quarter of the tomato mixture. Dribble a portion of the oil over each of the aubergines, pour a cup of water around them, and bake in a medium oven 375°F, 190°C, gas mark 5 for 35 to 40 minutes until the aubergines are cooked. Chop the parsley, fry the pine nuts gently in a smear of oil until they are light gold. To serve put an individual aubergine on each plate, sprinkle with parsley and put a quarter of the pine nuts over the top and serve immediately. If you are going to serve them cold, don't put pine nuts on until after the aubergines have cooled down completely.

FOR PHOTOGRAPH TURN TO PAGE 135.

PASTA 3x2

This is a very simple and quick dish to make which is as delightful to the eye as it is to the palate. It makes use of the wide range of multi-coloured pastas that are available in the shops today, the green ones are coloured and flavoured with spinach, the red ones are tomato and the gold ones are egg, and even when cooked they retain enough colour to set off the three vegetables that go with them in this dish ideally. Do follow the pasta cooking instructions: although they are not the ones you usually find on packs they work perfectly and in fact were developed nearly 20 years ago now by an Italian pasta firm which thought they were a much better way of cooking pasta with less energy and less waste, but except for crafty cooks they have never really caught on.

Attachments
Julienne cutter or coarse grater
thin slicer

Ingredients
1 lb (450 g) tricolori (or three coloured) pasta spirals
8 oz (225 g) each red peppers, courgettes and carrots
2 tablespoons olive oil
1 clove garlic
4 oz (100 g) Parmesan cheese
salt and pepper

Method
Peel and trim the carrots and then the courgettes, also trimmed into 1½ to 2 inch slices to fit horizontally in the feed-tube of your processor, cut the red peppers in half and carefully remove the seeds. Using the coarse julienne or big holed grater disc cut the courgettes and carrots into long thin strips, replace the disc with the slicing disc and slice the peppers. Peel, trim and crush the piece of garlic, put a pan with 2 pints of water on to boil with a pinch of salt and a drop of oil. When it comes to the boil add all the pastas, stir carefully, bring back to the boil for 3 minutes, switch off the heat completely put the lid on and leave. It will be cooked perfectly in 7 minutes and will last well for another 3 after that, just time enough for you to heat the oil in a large open frying pan or saucepan, add the crushed clove of garlic and fry for 1 minute, discard the garlic, add the carrots and red peppers and toss and turn over a high heat for 2 minutes, add the courgettes, turn again over a high heat, turn the heat down for 3 minutes and cover with a lid. To serve, drain the pasta thoroughly, pile it on a dish, stir the vegetables one last time, season generously and pile those on top of the pasta and add half the grated Parmesan and toss together. The remaining Parmesan is for individual diners to add some more cheese themselves. Do have a large peppermill on the table.

NUT ROAST

This is a very grand vegetarian course served on special occasions like Christmas or parties where something rather special and pretty looking is required. I use the vegetarian-based puff pastry that is available in all supermarkets these days but if you make your own puff pastry, or even rough puff pastry, that will do equally well. It is a dish to serve as though it were a piece of roast meat, that is with your favourite vegetables around it at Christmas time, sprouts, roast potatoes, mashed potatoes and perhaps even the cranberry sauce or apple sauce if you don't fancy the cranberries.

Attachment
double-bladed knife

Ingredients
8 oz (225 g) puff pastry
6 oz (175 g) wholemeal breadcrumbs
4 oz (100 g) brazil nuts
4 oz (100 g) chestnut purée (this can be bought in tins, but make sure you get one that isn't sweetened)
4 oz (100 g) button mushrooms
1 large onion
2 oz (50 g) fresh parsley
2 stalks celery
2 eggs

Method
Peel and trim all the vegetables and cut into 1 inch pieces. Trim the bread for the breadcrumbs of crusts and put into the processor and process until fine. Add the onions and celery and process them until also finely chopped. Add the nuts and mushrooms and process in 3 second bursts until roughly chopped, then add the chestnut purée, the eggs and herbs and seasonings and process in 2 or 3 more bursts until thoroughly blended. Roll the pastry out and use it to line a 2 lb loaf tin. Fill with the mixture and fold over the bottom, saving 2 or 3 scraps for subsequent decoration. Turn the tin out carefully onto a baking dish so that the folded over bits are underneath. Make the remaining bits of pastry into attractive leaves or other decorative shapes and fasten to the pastry with a beaten egg which you use to glaze the whole loaf with. Bake at 400°F, 200°C, gas mark 6 for 30 minutes, turn the heat down to 325°F, 170°C, gas mark 3 for another 15 minutes, making sure the pastry doesn't burn. Take out of the oven and, even if serving hot, allow to stand for 5 minutes to set before slicing like a loaf. It can also be served cold.

PASTITION

This is really a cross between moussaka and lasagne. It is a dish from the south eastern part of Italy where they still speak a form of Greek from when they were Greek colonies in classical times, and the west coast of Greece which has that natural connection with Italy and pasta. It is a very simple dish to make. It is very rich and filling because of the combination of sauces, vegetables and pasta.

Attachments
thick slicing disc
double-bladed knife

Ingredients
8 oz (225 g) aubergines
8 oz (225 g) courgettes
1 large onion
2 cloves garlic
1 tin Italian-style tomatoes
2 tablespoons thick Italian tomato purée
½ teaspoon basil
½ teaspoon oregano
8 oz (225 g) pasta shells or bows
2 eggs
5 oz (125 g) plain yoghurt
2 oz (50 g) olive oil (or ordinary cooking oil)
salt and pepper

Method
Trim the aubergines and courgettes and cut the aubergines in half lengthways so they fit in the feeder tube. Slice them and the courgettes, sprinkle on a tablespoon of salt and leave them, to get rid of any bitter taste, for 20 minutes. Meanwhile, chop the onion and garlic which you have peeled and trimmed (you can use the processor and knife blade for this), and fry them in the olive oil. Add the tin of tomatoes and the tomato purée and the herbs and season generously. Simmer for 20 minutes. Meanwhile, bring 2 pints (1 litre) of water to the boil, add a pinch of salt and a drop of oil and add the pasta. Leave to cook for 3 minutes, turn off and leave to stand for 7 to 8 minutes before draining. In a baking dish about 8 to 10 inches (20 to 25 cm) long and about 1½ inches (4 cm) deep, put half the tomato mixture then the aubergines and courgette slices which you have rinsed to get rid of the salt, then the rest of the tomato mixture, then the pasta and put to bake in a medium 350°F, 180°C, gas mark 4 oven for 45 minutes. You can, for extra richness, fry the aubergines and courgettes for 1 minute before laying them in the dish. Beat the eggs and yoghurt together and pour or spoon this over the top of the pasta and put back in the oven to bake for another 20 minutes until the coating is set. To serve, spoon out in portions making sure everybody gets a layer of egg and yoghurt sauce, pasta, the tomato sauce and the aubergines and courgettes. A wonderful dish to eat on its own or, surprisingly, with sauté potatoes.

SPINACH AND EGG LAYER CAKE

This is an unusual dish which makes a quite dramatic centrepiece as a main course. It is extremely filling and is one of those dishes that you never find in conventional meat cooking. It is layers of spinach, mornay sauce, and a nutmeg flavouring and very thinly cooked crisp omelettes. You can replace the omelettes if you like with homemade pancakes or even the kind of French ready-made pancakes you can buy in supermarkets. My own particular inclination though is for egg mixture, because it contains a high level of protein that you need to make sure a vegetarian diet is properly balanced.

Attachment
double-bladed knife

Ingredients
8 eggs
1½ lb (675 g) cooked spinach (frozen will do but it must be en branche)
1 sauce mornay (page 36)
½ teaspoon ground nutmeg
4 tablespoons grated Cheddar or Parmesan cheese
salt and pepper
cornflour

Method
Break the eggs into a bowl and pour into the processor with the double-bladed knife in, add a little cornflour and season generously and process until the mixture is thoroughly blended. Heat a large round, heavy frying pan, non-stick or conventional as you choose, and add just enough oil to prevent sticking. Put a small ladleful (about 4 tablespoons) of the omelette mixture into the pan, swirl it round to make sure it covers the bottom like a pancake and allow to set. Peel off carefully and put onto a plate. Put a piece of greaseproof paper on and repeat the process until you have five or six omelettes, depending on how thinly you pour in the mixture. Put half the recipe of mornay sauce in a saucepan, add the pre-cooked, roughly chopped spinach and stir thoroughly, add the nutmeg and season generously. On a large oven-proof dish put a pancake, a layer of spinach, another egg pancake, another layer of spinach and so on, until you have used up all the spinach and pancakes, finishing with a pancake on top. Pour on the remaining sauce as if you were icing a cake, spread it as much as you can down the sides. Don't worry too much about perfect covering. Sprinkle the cheese on top and bake for 25 minutes at 400°F, 200°C, gas mark 6 until the cheese has bubbled and browned. To serve, cut in wedges like a cake and lay sideways on a plate so that the striped effect of the spinach and egg is clearly visible. New potatoes and a non-green vegetable like carrots go very well with this.

1 **Pour the eggs into the bowl, add the cornflour, and season. Process until thoroughly blended.**

2 **Put a ladleful of mixture in a heated pan, swirl around, allow to set, and peel off carefully.**

3 Stack alternate layers of pancakes and spinach mixture, starting and ending with a pancake.

4 Pour on the remaining sauce, spreading down over the sides. Sprinkle the cheese on top.

TRY SPINACH AND EGG LAYER CAKE WITH NEW POTATOES AND CARROTS.

GUIDELINES ON GADGETS

All processors now come with a fairly comprehensive range of attachments as part of their kit, but most of them also provide for add-ons and additional gadgets that you can purchase separately or at the time you buy the processor. The better the processor the bigger the range of gadgets; though you may want to limit yourself to one or two at a time until you get used to them and see what use you can best make of them. This is a very brief guide to some of the more readily available sorts of gadgets that different manufacturers provide.

JUICE EXTRACTOR

This is, by and large, an attachment you will find really useful if your family is into a strong vegetarian style of eating or you grow an enormous number of your own vegetables and have gluts. What it does is effectively grate any fruit or vegetable so finely that it is reduced to juice and waste dry bulk. You can make surprisingly interesting and delicious combinations, cabbage and grape, carrot and apple, celery and beetroot. Anything you can eat raw you can turn into juice and I find it particularly useful at autumn harvest time when a huge number of apples, some of them damaged, can be trimmed and turned into lots of delicious juice.

CITRUS SQUEEZER

This is a kind of automated lemon or orange squeezer, sometimes supplied with two different sized centres to allow you to squeeze anything from a lime to a grapefruit. Once again it's the sort of tool that is most useful when you are processing a large amount of the appropriate fruit. If you do a lot of fresh orange juice then, without question, this is the tool for you. It is also possible to do some of the variety citrus juices, combinations of orange and lime or grapefruit and tangerine that you just can't buy in any shop.

MINI-BOWL

One range of processor in particular has brought out a really valuable development which is the mini-bowl. It is a small sized, almost cup sized miniature processor that fits inside the big bowl with its own tiny knife which allows you to process small quantities of things without dirtying the whole apparatus. It is ideal for making a small quantity of mayonnaise or chopping herbs or doing anything that requires close confinement and direct control.

Unusual Slicing Blades

There are a variety of these depending upon the manufacturer. Most processors come with a thin slicer and a medium grater but you can also buy wavy slicers which are great for potatoes or courgettes, although they are not so useful for the really softer vegetables like tomatoes or mushrooms. There are also the various sized chipping discs, from the julienne style that produces very fine but solid pieces of carrot or courgette to stir-fry or put into salads, to full size French fry style chips. The trick when using any of these is to get the vegetables you are going to cut up into a uniform size and shape that fits the feeding tube to its maximum, so you get the most efficient use of the cutters. If you make a lot of chips, or indeed salads or stir-frys, any or either of these discs are really useful. Many of the manufacturers also supply a thick slicer as well as a thin slicer for making potato dishes or cutting very thick slices of something like beetroot if you want to make a lot of pickles. They are also useful for cutting thick slices of orange peel, if you are into making marmalade. When you have squeezed the orange hard and got the pips out, pack the halves together in sets of 2 or 3 and push down the tube as one unit.

Liquidisers

Some processors also come with a liquidiser attachment which operates at a much higher speed with much smaller blades than the processor itself. I must admit I don't find them terribly useful as I find processors do almost everything I need at speeds I can control and manage, but if you are into milk shakes or soups or liquid mixes, and need the extra speed of the liquidiser, you may well find it very useful. It can also be used if you have had a problem with something like a mayonnaise separating to rescue the process without having to go through the laborious business of washing all the bowls again.

INDEX

Index

Index